Penguin Handbooks

The Dorset Coast Path

Hugh Westacott was born in London in 1932 and moved to Epsom, Surrey, on the outbreak of the war. He was educated at Tiffin Boys' School, Kingston-upon-Thames, and the North-Western Polytechnic. He was for ten years the Deputy County Librarian of Buckinghamshire and has also worked as a librarian in Sutton, Croydon, Sheffield, Bradford and Brookline, Massachusetts. During the war he spent his holidays with his family in Colyton, east Devon, walking five miles to the sea and back again each day, and his love of walking stems from these experiences. He is now a freelance writer and lecturer and in 1979 he was commissioned by Penguin to write this series of footpath guides to every national park and official long-distance path. He has also written *The Walker's Handbook* (Penguin, second edition 1980) and two forthcoming books, *Long Distance Paths: An International Directory* and *The Backpacker's Bible*. His other interests include the history of the Royal Navy in the eighteenth century and the writings of Evelyn Waugh. Hugh Westacott is married and has two daughters.

Mark Richards was born in 1949 in Chipping Norton, Oxfordshire. He was educated at Burford Grammar School before training for a farming career. He discovered the pleasures of hill walking through a local mountaineering club. He became friends with Alfred Wainwright, the creator of a unique series of pictorial guides to the fells of northern England, who encouraged him to produce a guide to the Cotswold Way, which was followed by guides to the North Cornish Coast Path and Offa's Dyke Path. For two years he produced a selection of hill walks for the *Climber and Rambler* magazine, and more recently he has contributed articles and illustrations to the *Great Outdoors* magazine and numerous walking books, culminating in the present series of Penguin footpath guides. As a member of various conservation organizations and a voluntary warden of the Cotswolds Area of Outstanding Natural Beauty, he is interested in communicating the need for the protection of environmental and community characteristics, particularly in rural areas. Mark Richards is happily married with two lively children, Alison and Daniel.

The Dorset Coast Path

H. D. Westacott

With maps by Mark Richards

Penguin Books

For my uncle,
Arthur Westacott

Penguin Books Ltd, Harmondsworth, Middlesex, England
Penguin Books, 625 Madison Avenue, New York, New York 10022, U.S.A.
Penguin Books Australia Ltd, Ringwood, Victoria, Australia
Penguin Books Canada Ltd, 2801 John Street, Markham, Ontario, Canada L3R 1B4
Penguin Books (N.Z.) Ltd, 182–190 Wairau Road, Auckland 10, New Zealand

First published 1982

Text copyright © H. D. Westacott, 1982
Maps copyright © Mark Richards, 1982
All rights reserved

Made and printed in Great Britain by
Richard Clay (The Chaucer Press) Ltd, Bungay, Suffolk
Set in Monophoto Univers

Contents

Acknowledgements

Many people have helped in the preparation of this guide. In particular I should like to thank Michael Douglas, the Rights of Way Officer for Dorset County Council, for much helpful information and for time and advice unstintingly given; the Postmasters and Postmistresses of Burton Bradstock, Chickerell, Chideock, Kimmeridge, Langton Herring, Overcombe, Osmington, Studland, West Bay and West Bexington for providing details of available facilities; Lieutenant Colonel R. G. Webber for advice on the section covering the Lulworth Firing Ranges; and Mr P. H. E. Carter of the South West Way Association for helpful information. I am grateful, too, for the letters received from walkers who have made corrections and helpful suggestions. The faults are mine alone.

Mark Richards has drawn the maps from my survey and I should like to express my deep appreciation for the superb job he has done and for the many valuable suggestions that he has made. The maps are based on the 1:25000 Ordnance Survey maps, with the sanction of the Controller of Her Majesty's Stationery Office (Crown copyright reserved).

Tribute must be paid to the many farmers and landowners who have cooperated so willingly to provide a fine coastal path.

Although every care has been taken in the preparation of this guide the author can accept no responsibility for those who stray from the Path.

Introduction

The Dorset Coast Path (long-distance path A1e) runs for 73 miles along the coast from the Devonshire border, just west of Lyme Regis, to Shell Bay, across the harbour from Bourne-mouth. From West Bexington to Osmington Mills there is a slightly shorter inland alternative route which reduces the total length to 66 miles. The Dorset Coast Path forms the last section of the South-West Peninsula Coast Path (long-distance path A1), also known as the South-West Way, which follows the coast for well over 600 miles from Minehead in Somerset via Land's End to Shell Bay in Dorset. It is the longest path in Britain and is more than twice as long as the Pennine Way (long-distance path D1). It has been devised and designated by the Countryside Commission. For much of its length it follows the path patrolled daily by the coastguard until the outbreak of the First World War.

The Dorset Coast Path was created to enable long-distance walkers to explore and enjoy the magnificent scenery of this section of coastline. The first 14 miles from Lyme Regis is very hilly and includes Golden Cap, which, at 618 ft, is the highest cliff on the south coast. From Burton Bradstock to Bowleaze Cove, just east of Weymouth, the route is flat for about 23 miles, but although there are no splendid seascapes, this section includes Chesil Beach and the Fleet and is full of interest for naturalists and those who enjoy the peculiar atmosphere of the saltings. At Abbotsbury the coastal section makes its only significant diversion inland to avoid the Swannery and the nature reserve. It is possible to avoid this flat section by taking the shorter inland alternative from West Bexington (mile 16) to Osmington Mills (mile 39), following the line of the Dorset Ridgeway. This alternative route has magnificent views across the sea and is of great interest to archaeologists because of the numerous prehistoric remains to be seen. The next 33 miles from Bowleaze Cove to Studland can only be described as magnificent and this section includes some of the finest scenery on the South-West Peninsula Coast Path. If the weather is kind, the walker will stride over the springy turf (and puff up the exceptionally steep hills!) revelling in the glorious combination of blue sky, white cliffs and the ever-changing colours of the sea.

Long-distance paths were established for pleasure, not for record-breaking purposes. Because our lives are governed by the need to conserve time, there is an unfortunate tendency to try to walk a route as quickly as possible. Unless you derive particular pleasure from testing yourself to the limit, take plenty of time and savour every moment of the walk. It is much better to be able to laze on the beach or cliff top, enjoying the sun and the distant sound of the surf, to pass the time of day with other walkers, to watch the wildlife and examine the flowers than to have the nagging urge to keep going at all costs in order to keep to a tight schedule. Experienced long-distance walkers know the value of Robert Louis Stevenson's much-quoted advice that 'To travel hopefully is a better thing than to arrive'. If you do not complete the whole route, you will not have 'failed' in any way at all, and there will be something to look forward to for another time.

It may come as a surprise to some to learn that parts of the Dorset Coast Path are very tough indeed. The final 33 miles from east of Bowleaze Cove are as arduous as any part of the Pennine Way. A glance at the path profiles at the bottom of the maps will show that it is quite normal to have two or three very steep descents and ascents in the 3 miles or so covered by the page. Remember, too, that every climb starts at sea level and goes to the top of the cliff, so there may be 1,200 to 1,500 ft of very steep climbing within the 3 miles. What goes up has to come down, so within the same distance will be a similar amount of descent. As every experienced walker knows, coming down a steep hill is probably more tiring than climbing it, especially with a heavy pack.

Planning the walk

When planning a walk along any long-distance path the walker has to make two decisions which will affect the course of all his future actions. The first decision is in which direction to walk the Path. The second is whether to make a series of day excursions or to walk the route in one expedition on consecutive days. Most people walk from west to east (Lyme Regis to Shell Bay), which means that they have the prevailing wind behind them.

Walkers who live some distance from the Path may find it difficult to walk in a series of day excursions, as the route is not conveniently served by motorways. However, it is perfectly feasible for strong walkers who are based in London to walk the Path in two long weekends by using public transport. On the first weekend, travel by train to Axminster, take the bus to Lyme Regis and walk as far as Weymouth (mile 34) to catch the train home on Sunday evening. On the second occasion, travel to Weymouth (mile 34) by train, walk to Shell Bay and take the bus into Bournemouth and the train back to London.

Walkers who prefer to stay in one place can walk the Path by using a combination of car and public transport providing they base themselves in Weymouth.

First day: Drive to West Bay (mile 11) and catch the Western National bus to Bridport. Change here for the bus to Lyme Regis and walk the 10 miles back to West Bay.

Second day: Drive to Abbotsbury (mile 20) and catch the Western National bus to West Bay (mile 11). Walk the 9 miles back to Abbotsbury.

Third day: From Weymouth catch the Western National bus to Abbotsbury (mile 20) and then walk the 14 flat miles to Weymouth.

Fourth day: From Weymouth walk the 11 miles to Lulworth Cove (mile 46), catch the Hants and Dorset bus to Wool station and then take the train back to Weymouth.

Fifth day: Drive to Lulworth Cove (mile 46), walk the 7 miles to Kimmeridge (mile 53) and then walk back to Lulworth Cove. Note that this is an arduous walk of 14 miles across the firing ranges (check that they are open).

Sixth day: (Thursday): Drive to Corfe Castle (not on the Path) and catch South Dorset Coaches service to Kimmeridge. Walk the 12 miles to Swanage (mile 65) and catch the Hants and Dorset bus to Corfe Castle. (*The South Dorset Coaches service operates on Thursdays only.*)

Seventh day: Drive to Swanage (mile 65) and walk the 8 miles to Shell Bay (mile 73). Catch the Hants and Dorset bus to Swanage.

Between West Bexington (mile 16) and Osmington Mills (mile 39) there is now an inland alternative which avoids

Weymouth and one of the least attractive sections of the coast. The inland alternative is 16 miles long (compared with 23 miles covered by those who follow the coast) and is a high-level route following the Dorset Ridgeway with splendid views of the sea. In my view, the inland alternative is much more attractive scenically, although ornithologists and those who enjoy the saltings may prefer to keep to the coast. The route of the inland alternative is shown on pp. 80–91.

Hazards and difficulties

Those who know the Dorset coastline only from lazing on its beaches may be surprised to learn that they may encounter dangers along the route. One of the remarkable features of the Path is that considerable sections now lie beneath the sea! This is because many of the cliffs are subject to erosion and are constantly falling. Keep away from the cliff edge, or that splendid view may be your last, and on no account ever attempt to climb the cliff face, as the surface is unstable and friable.

The line of the Path is usually clear, but walkers may experience some difficulty if a mist rolls in from the sea. No one who has not experienced this phenomenon can have any idea how frightening and disorientating it can be. Suddenly, and often with very little warning, the Path ahead disappears and all sense of direction is lost. On the less frequented sections the novice can find the experience alarming and chastening.

Gales, too, can be a hazard on the more exposed sections of the Path. A walker dressed in cagoule and overtrousers and carrying a large pack presents so much windage that at times it is difficult to keep a proper balance. I was once so frightened by the way that I was stumbling near the cliffs that I left the coast and retreated inland until the wind had moderated.

Perhaps a more welcome hazard (because it requires fine weather) is the risk of sunburn. On a fine day the walker will receive several hours' exposure to sunlight, which will be magnified by reflection from the sea and the white cliffs. It is important to acclimatize slowly until a good tan has been acquired. Wind can burn the skin as painfully as can the sun, and it is a good plan to carry some salve to help to prevent the lips from chapping and cracking. During the very hot summer of 1976 a number of walkers suffered from dehydration. Some actually had to be rescued on farm trailers and hosed down to restore their body fluids.

In dry weather the surface of the Path is likely to be firm, but after heavy rain some of the chalk slopes on the steep hills will be slippery and treacherous, and the section around Abbotsbury (mile 20) may be ankle-deep in mud.

Lulworth firing ranges

The army uses the most beautiful stretch of the Dorset coast between Lulworth Cove (mile 46) and Kimmeridge (mile 53) as a firing range which is open to the public only at certain times. Note that access to this stretch of the Path is by permission: it is *not* a public right of way. Walkers must time their arrival at the range when it is open, otherwise they will be faced with a 12-mile walk to Kimmeridge along roads. The army has waymarked the 6-mile route with posts placed at 100-yd intervals. About 70,000 shells are fired each year, which means that the Path must be searched before it is opened to ensure that no high-explosive shells are left. *It is absolutely essential to observe the following rules:*

Never enter the ranges if the gate is locked
Never stray from the path
Never allow children or dogs to stray
Never enter any building
Never pick up any object
Never camp or light fires
Never attempt the walk if there is a mist
Never enter the ranges unless you have plenty of time to complete the very arduous 6-mile walk
ALWAYS obey the instructions of the range wardens

As it is forbidden (and dangerous) to stray from the line of the Path, walkers are advised, in the interests of modesty, to go to the loo *before* entering the ranges.

The exact dates that the ranges are open vary slightly from year to year and the following information is given as an indication only:

Every Saturday and Sunday except for about six weeks each year
One week at Easter

One week at the Spring Bank Holiday
From the beginning of August to mid-September
Two weeks at Christmas and the New Year

The exact dates are published in local newspapers and the current edition of the *South West Coastal Path Guide*, published annually by the South West Way Association (see p. 16). Information can be obtained from the Range Officer, R A C Centre, Bovington Camp, Wareham, Dorset; tel. Bindon Abbey (0929) 462721 ext. 859.

Maps, timetables and accommodation

Although this guide contains all the information necessary to follow the route of the Dorset Coast Path, many walkers will want to arm themselves with additional information. It is very helpful to have a map which will set the Path within the context of the surrounding countryside. Three sheets of the 1:50000 Ordnance Survey map cover the whole route — numbers 193, 194 and 195. However the 1:100000 Bartholomew map sheet number 4 covers the whole of Dorset and the Coast Path is marked on it. This map lacks the detail of the Ordnance Survey maps but is perfectly adequate when used in conjunction with this guide, saving both weight and money. Some walkers find that a cheap motoring map published by one of the oil companies is perfectly adequate.

Rural bus services are subject to change, withdrawal and reduction. Furthermore, some of them are seasonal and any walker planning to use public transport will be well advised to obtain beforehand copies of the relevant timetables. The Somerset and Dorset edition of the Western National Bus Company contains details of all bus services (including independent operators) and train services in the western half of the county. Public transport in the eastern half of the county is detailed in the timetables of the Hants and Dorset Bus Company. Both timetables are available by post from The Bus Station, The Square, Bournemouth. Prices and postage costs are unpredictable, so it is advisable to send a cheque made out to the Hants and Dorset Bus Company but without completing the details for the amount.

There is plenty of accommodation in the main tourist centres of Lyme Regis (mile 1), Charmouth (mile 3), Weymouth (mile 34) and Swanage (mile 66), but it is scarcer elsewhere.

Advanced booking is advised and is probably essential in the main tourist season from mid-July to mid-September. The South West Way Association has a useful accommodation list in its annual handbook (see p. 16). Accommodation lists published by commercial interests, tourist boards and the publicity departments of local authorities can be consulted at most large public libraries throughout the country.

Youth Hostels are located at Bridport (about $1\frac{1}{2}$ miles inland from Eype Mouth – between miles 9 and 10 – and 2 miles inland from West Bay – mile 11), Litton Cheney (3 miles inland from West Bexington – mile 16) and Swanage (mile 66).

Authorized camping sites are plentiful on the route of the Path. Walkers should note that they have no right to camp anywhere, not even on the beach, without first obtaining the permission of the landowner.

Kit and equipment

Experienced walkers know that there is nothing to beat well-broken-in boots for comfort on a long walk. They will be found especially useful on the muddy sections around Abbotsbury (mile 20) and along the Fleet (between miles 24 and 33), where the Path may be waterlogged. However, stout shoes with two pairs of socks will suffice. Track shoes and canvas boots are not suitable, especially if a heavy pack is being carried, as they may disintegrate on some of the steep hills.

In summer, wear cotton underclothes, breeches or loose cotton trousers and a cotton T-shirt or light woollen sweater. Shorts may be suitable in fine weather, but do beware of sunburn and ensure a healthy tan *before* starting the walk. A cagoule and nylon overtrousers, if you have them, are useful for foul weather, but a plastic mac and overtrousers will serve. Do not wear jeans, as they are too tight and miserably cold and clinging when wet.

All gear should be carried in a comfortable, well-fitting rucksack.

Food and water

It is essential that all walkers should carry plenty of water, as many of the cafés are seasonal and may not be open. Water can be drawn from public conveniences, which are marked on the maps, and begged from cafés and public houses which you have patronized. If the loos do not have a drinking water tap, draw water from the wash basin and add some water-purifying tablets just in case it is not from the mains.

It is also wise to carry sufficient food to last for at least a day, and more if backpacking. The towns and villages which have grocer's shops are mentioned in the text.

How to use the guide

The purpose of this guide is to provide all the information that the walker requires to enable him to walk the route of the Dorset Coast Path, either from the east or from the west. The main body of the guide comprises twenty-five strip maps of the route on a scale of 1:25000 (approximately $2\frac{1}{2}$ ins. to the mile), which show the route in very great detail, including information such as the location of gates, stiles, signposts and waymarks which the Ordnance Survey do not show on their maps. Although based on the Ordnance Survey maps (with the sanction of the Controller of Her Majesty's Stationery Office), they have been updated by means of personal survey and are thus more accurate. Six further maps cover the alternative route between West Bexington and Osmington Mills.

A great deal of thought has gone into the design of the maps and they must be studied carefully in conjunction with the key in order to get the most from them. To reduce the amount of unnecessary detail and to avoid cluttering them unduly, contour and grid lines have been omitted. Instead, grid line numbers form the frame of each map, so that it is possible to relate them to any Ordnance Survey map and to use a compass, if required. Instead of indicating heights in the conventional way, a profile of the Path is shown in half scale at the bottom of every map. The numbers in the path profile relate to the mile numbers given on the map. In this way it is possible to see at a glance whether the section of the route to be walked is easy or strenuous.

It has already been said that the guide can be used in either direction. North, although always indicated, is of academic interest only and is not usually on this route, at the top of the page. The guide is designed to be held in a natural reading position in front of the walker. Those travelling eastward, towards Shell Bay, start at the front of the guide and their eyes follow the route *up* the page. Wayfarers travelling westward, towards Lyme Regis, start at the back of the guide and their eyes go *down* the page. The only disadvantage that those travelling west will be under is that the text will have to be read in reverse order (paragraph by paragraph, *not* word by word!).

Opposite every map is the relevant section of text. Here will be found brief notes of interesting things to be seen along the way and, wherever route-finding is difficult, a description of the route to supplement the map. Information given in the text includes the location of shops, banks, post offices, cafés, restaurants, public houses and accommodation. Early closing days are given together with brief details of the availability of public transport.

Great care has been taken in the compilation of this guide, but walkers should be aware that the countryside is constantly changing and that time may render parts of this guide out of date. In particular, vandals may vent their wrath on waymarks and signposts. The author would be most grateful for comments and criticisms as well as information about changes which have made the guide out of date. (Please write c/o Penguin Books Ltd, 536 King's Road, London SW10 0UH.) Neither the author nor the publisher can accept any responsibility for the consequences incurred if the wayfarer departs from the right of way.

The South West Way Association

The South West Way Association was formed to promote the interests of users of the South-West Peninsula Coast Path, of which the Dorset Coast Path is a part. It invites all with an interest in the coast paths of the south-west to join.

The Association publishes a series of maps and guides to certain sections of the Path and an annual handbook somewhat misleadingly entitled *The South West: A Complete Guide to the Coastal Path*. It is *not* a complete guide in the sense that this guide is; nevertheless it is essential reading for anyone planning to walk any section of the Path, as it contains a large amount of up-to-date information about such things as temporary diversions, cliff falls, public transport, ferries and accommodation.

Inquiries about membership and the sale of publications should be made to: Mrs M. MacLeod, 1 Orchard Drive, Kingskerswell, Newton Abbot, Devon.

Tourist Information Centres

Advice and assistance in booking accommodation may be obtained from the following information centres situated on or near the coast:

Bridport: 32 South Street; tel. (0308) 24901.
Dorchester: Antelope Yard, South Street; tel. (0305) 67922.
Lyme Regis: The Guildhall, Bridge Street; tel. (029 74) 2138.
Swanage: Room 1, Shore Road; tel. (092 92) 2885.
Weymouth: The Esplanade; tel. (0305) 785747.

Geology

The geology of the Dorset coastline is complicated. The basic rock between Lyme Regis and West Bay is Liassic. The Blue Lias, which is found at sea level, is very rich in fossils and is overlaid with other Liassic rocks and topped with various kinds of sandstone. From West Bay to Burton Bradstock the cliffs are formed of Bridport Sands overlaid with Oolitic Limestone. The flat section of the Path from Burton Cliff to Overcombe, west of Weymouth, is formed of Oxford clays and Cornbrash. Portland Bill is virtually solid limestone. Next comes the chalk, which gives way to Kimmeridge Clay, an oily shale. West of Kimmeridge are the Purbeck Beds consisting of limestone which stretches as far as Swanage. The chalk reappears briefly near Studland.

Archaeology

Dorset is particularly rich in archaeological remains and even those with little concern for the distant past cannot fail to notice the imprint that early man has made on the landscape.

Britain became an island about 8,000 years ago, when the sea broke through the narrow isthmus which joined us to continental Europe. During this period our forefathers were mesolithic hunters and fishers who wandered about the Isle of Purbeck and the flat lands behind Chesil Beach, hunting their prey. They have left a few sites of consuming interest to archaeologists but no visible remains for the casual observer. They possessed fire and primitive stone axes and with these tools they started the long process of clearing the primeval forest.

Somewhere about the year 3500 B C came the first wave of neolithic invaders from the continent. They brought with them such skills as pottery making and farming and they were also traders. During this period most of the downland was cleared of forest to provide grazing for their semi-domesticated animals. They built a considerable number of huge long barrows and burial mounds and the huge hill fort at Maiden Castle, which was later improved in the Iron Age.

An influx of Bronze Age people occurred in about 2000 B C. They brought with them metal tools which were far superior to the flint implements of the previous culture. Of all the prehistoric people, it is they who have left the clearest mark on the landscape, for they were mostly responsible for constructing the numerous barrows and burial mounds which are such a feature of the Dorset landscape. Most examples are to be found on the chalk, but it must not be assumed that this was their only or even their most important habitat. By this time, Dorset was quite densely populated and the Bronze Age sites in the more fertile parts of Dorset have largely been obliterated by more recent settlements, leaving those on the less attractive farming areas of the chalk for us to see.

The next wave of invaders were the Iron Age people and it is they who built most of the hill forts. Two examples lie near the Coast Path at Flowers Barrow near mile 49 and at Abbotsbury Castle on the inland section just east of West Bexington. Maiden Castle, which was built by the neolithic people of the Windmill Hill culture, was strengthened and improved during the Iron Age.

The Romans had a profound influence on Dorset, although there is not very much left for us to see. Vespasian stormed Maiden Castle with the Augusta Legion in AD 45 and inflicted a crushing defeat on the Celtic tribes, which was repeated at Hod Hill and Spettisbury. Three hundred years of the remarkable Pax Romana descended upon Dorset – the Romans, with their genius for governing and keeping order, were quite content to let the tribes retain their own way of life provided they paid their taxes and did not make a nuisance of themselves. The Romans built the important city of Durnovaria, the modern Dorchester, almost under the ramparts of Maiden Castle, and constructed villas throughout the county. Most of the Roman remains have disappeared under the modern town, but one of the most complete Roman town houses in Britain can be seen in Colliton Park and there are many interesting exhibits in the Dorchester Museum. The ancient henge monument of Maumbury Rings, just outside Dorchester, was converted by the Romans into an amphitheatre.

With the collapse of the Empire and the withdrawal of Roman troops from Britain, the Romano-British maintained their way of life and it took a long time before Saxon influence was brought to bear on Dorset. This seems to be because the inhabitants vigorously defended their way of life and there is strong evidence to suppose that the crushing defeat suffered by the Saxons at Mount Badon about the year AD 500 took place at Badbury Rings. It was not until AD 665 that the Saxons occupied Dorchester.

Agriculture and Industry

For centuries agriculture and fishing have been the mainstay of Dorset, the most rural of counties, and there is little evidence of industrial disfigurement. Both Portland stone and Purbeck marble have been quarried for centuries, but the only significant scars are on a small area of Portland Bill. During the Middle Ages, Portland stone was used in the construction of the Tower of London, Westminster Palace and Exeter Cathedral and during the seventeenth century both Inigo Jones and Christopher Wren used the material extensively. Until the railway reached Portland towards the end of the last century the stone was shipped by sea. Purbeck marble, which was also transported in ships, was used in the construction of Westminster Abbey and the Cathedrals of Exeter, Winchester, Wells, Worcester and Salisbury, as well as in countless parish churches up and down the land.

Clay has been extracted from the Isle of Purbeck and various attempts have been made to exploit the shale of the Kimmeridge clay beds. The only really successful result has been the extraction of oil in recent years and there is a strong possibility that we shall see off-shore drilling in the not too distant future. Bridport once had a flourishing rope-making industry. Agriculture and tourism are probably the two most important industries at the present time.

Wildlife

Because of its complicated geological structure, Dorset has a wide variety of habitats which support a very diversified wildlife. There is some industry around Poole, and Weymouth and Swanage have spread themselves along the coast, but on the whole the county still remains remarkably rural in character. Furthermore, the area occupied by the army's firing ranges at Lulworth has remained free from the herbicides and pesticides which have had such a detrimental effect on the delicate balance of nature in most rural areas.

The most obvious form of wildlife are the birds. In addition to the ubiquitous gulls which will be found wherever there are cliffs and beaches, the observant wayfarer is likely to see stonechats, jackdaws and kestrels throughout the length of this coastline. The Fleet provides breeding grounds for little terns, reed buntings, reed warblers, ringed plovers and many species of waders and wildfowl. There is a colony of cormorants at Old Harry Rocks near Studland, and from Portland Bill during the migratory season can be seen gannets, terns, razorbills, shearwaters, skuas and many more. There have been some very unusual sightings. The peregrine falcon once bred at Gad Cliff and are sometimes still to be seen near Abbotsbury Swannery. The rarest bird, unique to Dorset, is the Dartford warbler, which is now restricted to the National Nature Reserve at Studland. Here, too, may be seen the hobby, the marsh harrier, water rails and many varieties of wildfowl.

The only mammals likely to be seen in any number are rabbits and hares (the latter have even been sighted on Chesil Beach), but their predators, the fox, badger, weasel and stoat, though common, are more reluctant to show themselves. The otter is reputed still to fish for eels in the Little Sea in the National Nature Reserve at Studland, which also has a colony of roe deer. Deer may also be seen in the woods and heaths of the inland section of the Path.

Hardy's Egdon Heath, described so vividly in the opening chapter of *The Return of the Native*, has almost entirely disappeared except for the small area which comprises the Studland Heath National Nature Reserve. The birds and mammals likely to be found here have been mentioned above and it is also the habitat of the marsh orchid, the carnivorous sundew, bog asphodel, bogbean and bog pimpernel. It is one of the last refuges of the smooth snake and the sand lizard.

The chalk hills around Lulworth support many varieties of butterfly, including the very rare Lulworth skipper, graylings, chalkhill blues, the dark green fritillary and the marbled white. Ballard Down is another rich habitat for butterflies.

Among the innumerable varieties of wild flowers and plants, mention should be made of some of the less common species including samphire, sea kale, wild cabbage, sea holly, sea campion and horned poppy. On the limestone can be found the rare spider orchid as well as bee orchids. In spring, the ubiquitous sea pink can be found throughout the length of the coastline.

Thomas Hardy

No guide to Dorset can avoid mentioning Thomas Hardy. Of all 'regional novelists' he had the greatest sense of place and local landscape. Most of the settings of his novels can be readily identified and we know the real names of the locations he hides under his fictitious Wessex names.

He was born at Higher Bockhampton in 1840 and apart from short periods of residence in London he lived most of his life in Dorset. He was a dramatist and major poet, but it is as a novelist that his feelings for and his description of the Dorset landscape are best revealed.

Like Wordsworth's, his work is of uneven quality, and some of the novels dealing with middle-class themes are much inferior to his best work. He was not a great literary stylist, but he excelled at describing landscapes and his characters were much buffeted by the slings and arrows of outrageous fortune. He was greatly concerned with the plight of the agricultural labourer and was adept at describing the minutiae of their lives, their hopes and aspirations. These humble people often acted as a kind of Greek chorus to the main events of the novels. His best fiction includes *Under the Greenwood Tree, Far from the Madding Crowd, The Return of the Native, The Trumpet-Major, The Mayor of Casterbridge, The Woodlanders, Tess of the d'Urbervilles* and *Jude the Obscure*. He also wrote several volumes of short stories.

No major events from the novels occur on the coast, but those who decide to walk the inland section from West Bexington to Osmington Mills will pass very close to Sutton Poyntz, the Overcombe of *The Trumpet-Major*.

Book List

Allsop, Kenneth, *In the Country,* Hamish Hamilton, 1972.

Benfield, Eric, *Dorset,* Robert Hale, 1950.

Bettey, J. H., *Dorset* (City and County Histories), David & Charles, 1974.

Bond, L. M. G., *Tyneham: A Lost Heritage,* Friary Press, 1955.

Davies, G. M., *The Dorset Coast,* A. & C. Black, 1956.

Fagersten, Anton, *The Place Names of Dorset,* E P Publishing, 1978.

Farr, Grahame, *Wreck and Rescue on the Dorset Coast,* D. Bradford Barton Ltd., 1971.

Geologists' Association, Guide 22, *Poole to the Chesil Beach,* and Guide 23, *Branscombe to Burton Bradstock,* Benham and Co.

Jackman, Brian, *Dorset Coast Path,* H M S O, 1979.

Legg, Rodney, *Purbeck Isle,* Dorset Publishing Co., 1972.

Mee, Arthur, *Dorset,* Hodder & Stoughton, 1967.

Pevsner, Nikolaus, *Dorset* (Buildings of England), Penguin Books, 1972.

Pinion, F. B., *A Hardy Companion: A Guide to the Works of Thomas Hardy and the Background,* Macmillan, 1976.

Pitt-Rivers, Michael, *Dorset: A Shell Guide,* Faber & Faber, 1966.

South West Way Association, *The South West Way: A Complete Guide to the Coastal Path,* published annually.

Steers, J. A., *The Sea Coast* (New Naturalist Series), 4th edn, Collins, 1969.

Taylor, Christopher, *Dorset* (The Making of the English Landscape), Hodder & Stoughton, 1970.

Timperley, H. W. and Brill, Edith, *Ancient Trackways of Wessex,* Dent, 1965.

Ward, Kenneth and Mason, John, *The South-West Peninsula Coast Path,* Vol. 3, Plymouth to Poole, 2nd edn, Letts, 1980.

Ward, Lock, *Dorset and Wiltshire.*

Guide and Sectional Maps

The Dorset Coast Path

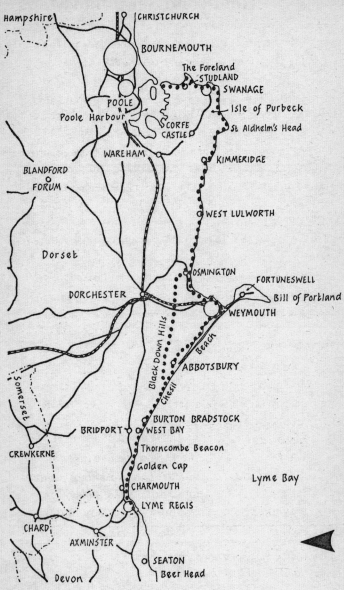

KEY

• • • • • Coast Path   • • • • Practical wading route

———————— Coast Path on metalled surface

(41)   Distance in miles from Lyme Regis

• • • • •   Other visible paths or tracks

⸺ Hedge ⸺ Wall ⸺ Barbed fence

Trees or Woodland ⸺ Plain fence

⸺ Cliff or steep seaward slope

Low Water Mark (only shown at fordable estuaries)

High Water Mark ⸺ Bushes

Marshy ground ⸺ Stream with direction

÷ Tumulus   Footbridge ⸺ of flow

⸺ Earthwork

✝ Church ▲ Youth Hostel 🗼 Lighthouse or Beacon

▪▪ Buildings (only shown to assist navigation)

wc: Public Conveniences cg: Coast Guard Lookout Post

⸺ Major road ⸺ Minor road

———————— Other road ⸺ Railway

— — — — — — — — — — — — — Ferry Service

⸺●⸺ Railway station ✚ Bus station

c : Coast Path sign

B : Bridleway sign

D : Double (as in double gate)   Direction
                                      of North

F : Footpath sign

FB : Footbridge   [A] Refers to note on facing page

17   G : Gate   The numbers in the margin   17

K : Kissing Gate   locate the Northings and

S : Stile   Eastings (Grid Lines) on

W : Waymark   Ordnance Survey maps

05   04

Contour profile of route showing   91 ⸺
milepoints and height in metres
                                              41

29

1. Devonshire Head, Lyme Regis, Charmouth

3½ miles
Maps: 1:25000 sheet SY29/39; 1:50000 sheet 193
Terrain: From Devonshire Head the Path is well used to Lyme Regis.
There follows a stretch of main road walking and then the Path
climbs over the cliffs.

The official start of the Dorset Coast Path is Devonshire Head, but most wayfarers will begin their walk at Lyme Regis.

From Lyme Regis take the busy A3052 road towards Charmouth and look for the unsignposted path on the right-hand side of the road opposite the cemetery. A kissing gate leads into a field.

At point A, east-bound walkers must turn left on reaching the lane and walk almost to the gate across it, then take the narrow path on the right which climbs up through the trees. Those going west must turn left on reaching the lane and then take the stile on the right.

When the tide is falling it is possible to walk along the firm sand between Lyme Regis and Charmouth.

Lyme Regis (population 3,500) has shops, cafés, restaurants, public houses, banks, a post office, accommodation, campsites and buses to Axminster, Bridport, Charmouth, Dorchester, Sidmouth, Seaton and Weymouth. From Axminster there are trains to Exeter and London. Early closing day is Thursday.

It is an attractive old town and is one of the 'loyal and ancient boroughs' in Britain. It was granted a charter in 774 by Cynewulf and is mentioned in the Domesday Book. During the Middle Ages it was an important sea port. During the Civil War, Lyme was fortified by the parliamentary forces, endured a siege of two months in 1644 and was relieved by the Earl of Essex. In 1685 the Duke of Monmouth landed on the Cobb in a vain attempt to claim the English throne. Within a few days he mustered an army of 5,000, but it was a lost cause and, after his defeat at Sedgemoor, 12 Lyme men who had participated in the rebellion were hanged on the spot where Monmouth had landed.

The Cobb, the old stone pier which forms the harbour, is lined with quaint shops and there is a marine aquarium on Victoria Pier. The parish church of St Michael the Archangel is mainly sixteenth-century but has a thirteenth-century tower and is built on three levels. In a display case in the chancel is a chained copy of a Breeches Bible and a Bad Bible. The Philpot Museum contains an extensive collection of fossils from the surrounding cliffs, from which the study of palaeontology in this country first started. Buddle Bridge is surrounded by attractive streets and buildings.

Lyme was a particular favourite of Jane Austen when she spent her summer holidays here. It was here that she wrote *Persuasion* and it was on the Cobb that Louisa Musgrove fell.

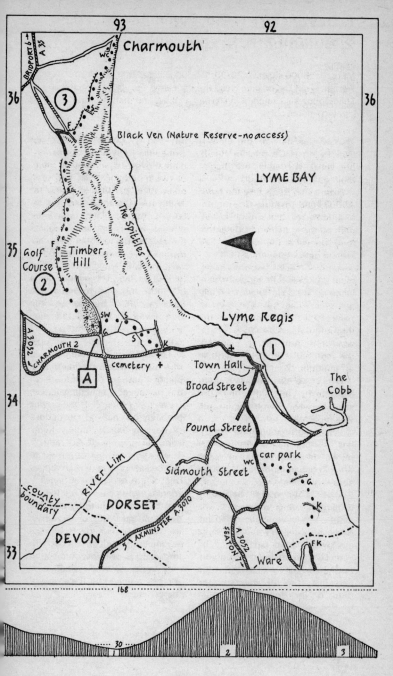

2. Charmouth, St Gabriel's Mouth

3 miles
Maps: 1:25000 sheet SY29/39; 1:50000 sheet 193
Terrain: A steep climb over the National Trust property
Stonebarrow Hill, using well-marked paths.

At Broom Cliff, between miles 5 and 6, the route waymarked by the National Trust is shown. This differs slightly from the official route, which goes further inland and is hardly ever used.

Charmouth (population 1,000) has shops, cafés, restaurants, public houses, a bank, a post office, accommodation, campsites and buses to Axminster, Lyme Regis and Weymouth. Early closing day is Thursday. When the tide is falling it is possible to walk to Lyme Regis along the firm sand of the beach.

Conies Castle, an ancient earthwork a little to the north of Charmouth, is reputed to have been the camp of a Saxon King Egbert when he fought the Danes in AD 833. According to the *Anglo-Saxon Chronicle*, 'King Egbert fought against the men of the 35 ships at Charmouth and it was great slaughter made and the Danish men maintained the position of the field.'

Jane Austen was enchanted by Charmouth and wrote of it: 'Its high grounds and extensive sweeps of country and still more its sweet retired bay backed by dark cliffs where fragments of low rock among the sands make it the happiest spot for watching the flow of the tide, for sitting in unwearied contemplation, the wooded variety the cheerful village of Uplyme; a scene so wonderful and so lovely as may more than equal any of the resembling scenes of the far famed Isle of Wight, these places must be visited and visited again.' Charmouth was the home of Mary Anning, an amateur geologist, who in 1811, when only 12 years old, uncovered the skeleton of a 21-foot-long ichthyosaurus in a near-by cliff. In her twenties she discovered the fossilized remains of a plesiosaurus and a pterodactyl.

The Old Bridge at the east end of the town has a plaque threatening transportation for life to anyone caught damaging it. The Queens Armes Hotel was probably originally a guest house of near-by Forde Abbey. Katherine of Aragon stayed here in 1501 and her coat-of-arms can still be seen in the plasterwork of one of the bedrooms. Charles II spent a night here when attempting to leave the country after his defeat at the Battle of Worcester in 1651. The George Hotel is a seventeenth-century coaching inn with a window projecting over the porch from which passengers watched for the arrival of the coach.

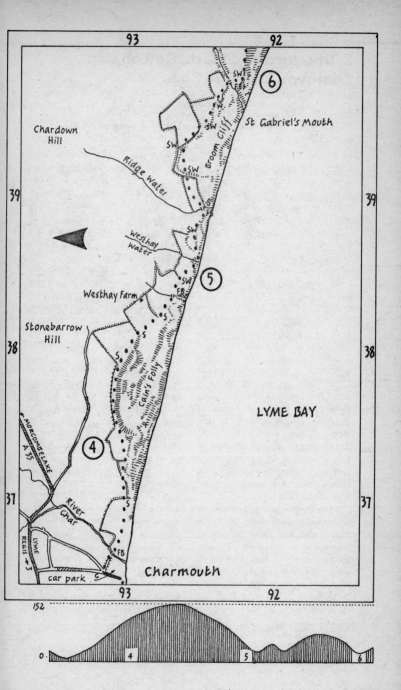

3. St Gabriel's Mouth, Golden Cap, Seatown, East Ebb Cove

2½ miles
Maps: 1:25000 sheet SY49/59; 1:50000 sheet 193
Terrain: Some very strenuous cliff walking with steep gradients and splendid views.

Golden Cap, the highest coastal cliff on the south coast, is 618 ft high, and has views to match. It gets its name from the sandy gravel near the summit, which gives it its characteristic colour. When seen from a distance in the setting rays of the sun it shimmers like gold.

Seatown is full of caravans and has a grocer's shop, a public house and a campsite.

On the eastern side of Seatown the Path goes through the car park.

Chideock (pronounced Chiddick), a mile inland from Seatown, has a grocer's shop, public houses, a post office and accommodation. There is a bus service to Axminster, Lyme Regis, Weymouth and Bridport. Early closing day is Wednesday.

The parish church of St Giles, mainly Perpendicular, was extensively damaged in the Civil War. The Arundell Chapel contains the splendid black marble tomb of Sir John Arundell, with an effigy depicting him in full plate armour. To the north-east of the church are the remains of the castle mound, on which stands a simple cross with a plaque. This states that the castle was built by Sir John de Chideock in 1380 and was taken and destroyed by the Parliamentary forces in 1645. The Chideocks were staunch Catholics and during Elizabethan times harboured priests. Five Catholics were taken from the castle and executed. The Manor House was built at the beginning of the nineteenth century. In the grounds is the Victorian Roman Catholic Chapel of Our Lady of Martyrs and Saint Ignatius. This is very Byzantine in character and the sacristy and the loft have frescoes on the walls and ceilings.

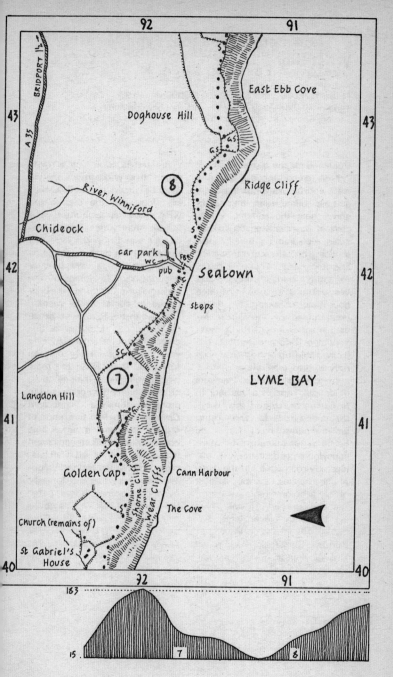

BRIDPORT 1¼

A 35

43

92   91

East Ebb Cove

Doghouse Hill

GS

GS

⑧

River Winniford

Ridge Cliff

S

Chideock

car park

WC

pub

42

Seatown

steps

SC

⑦

LYME BAY

Langdon Hill

41

Golden Cap

Cann Harbour

Shorre Cliff

Wear Cliffs

The Cove

Church (remains of)

St Gabriel's House

40

92   91

183

15   7   8

4. Thorncombe Beacon, Eype Mouth, West Bay

2½ miles
Maps: 1:25000 sheet SY49/59; 1:50000 sheet 193
Terrain: A relatively easy stretch with just one stiff climb.

At Eype Mouth the Path crosses the stream by means of some steps and stepping stones.

Eype (pronounced Eep), just off the Path, has a public house, a post office, accommodation and a campsite.

West Bay has a grocer's shop, cafés, restaurants, public houses, a post office, accommodation and a campsite. There are buses to Long Bredy, Bridport and Weymouth. West Bay must have been charming, but it has been ruined by insensitive development. Originally it was known as Bridport Harbour, but it has silted up and is now used only by pleasure craft.

Eastward-travelling walkers must walk round the harbour to reach the beach and then climb the cliff at the far end. Those walking west must leave the beach by the obvious exit.

Bridport (population 6,500) has shops, cafés, restaurants, public houses, banks, a post office, accommodation, a campsite and a Youth Hostel. There are buses to Lyme Regis, Axminster, Beauminster, West Bay, Burton Bradstock, Dorchester and Weymouth. There are train services to London (Paddington and Waterloo), Bristol and Dorchester.

Bridport is an attractive town. Much flax was grown in the neighbourhood and was woven into ropes on the rope walks which were set up in the town — hence the wide streets. So famous was Bridport's rope that the expression 'to be stabbed by a Bridport dagger' was used as a euphemism for hanging. The rope-making tradition is continued in some of the modern factories in the town. The parish church of St Mary is a fine church, mainly Perpendicular in style, but with Early English transepts. There is an old tomb with an effigy of a knight sitting cross-legged which is reputed to represent John de Chideock, a Crusader. The Museum and Art Gallery houses an interesting collection of exhibits on rope-making as well as local archaeology and natural history, Victoriana and agriculture and domestic bygones. Thomas Hardy called the town Port Bredy in his novels and used it as a setting for scenes in *Tess of the d'Urbervilles, The Mayor of Casterbridge, The Woodlanders* and some of the short stories.

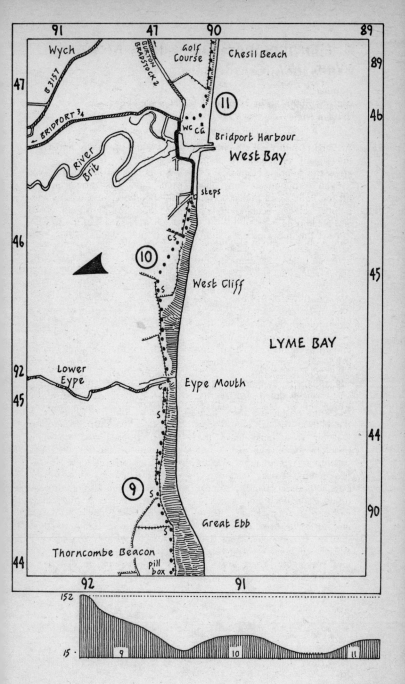

5. East Cliff, Burton Freshwater, Burton Bradstock, Cogden Beach

2½ miles
Maps: 1:25000 sheets SY49/59 and SY58; 1:50000 sheets 193 and 194
Terrain: A steep climb up from West Bay over East Cliff, followed by a long flat section.

At Burton Freshwater the official route follows the fence round the edge of the golf course to reach the footbridge by keeping inland of the caravans. A more direct route is shown, and at low tide it is possible to ford the stream where it crosses the beach. There are water taps on the caravan site.

Burton Bradstock, just off the Path, has a grocer's shop, a café, public houses, a post office, accommodation, a campsite and buses to Bridport and Weymouth.

It is an exceptionally pretty village with many thatched cottages and a village green. The parish church of St Mary is mainly Perpendicular, with an embattled central tower and seventeenth-century communion rails. The clock came from Christ's Hospital. It once had two thriving local industries. Flax was grown and spun into ropes and nets in the local mill. Fishing was also very important, but the fleet is now much reduced. At one time there were no less than fourteen public houses in the village (there are now three).

This section sees the start of Chesil Beach, a ridge of pebbles formed by the action of the sea, which runs for 18 miles to Portland. Bathing is extremely dangerous throughout its length, as there is a strong undertow.

The 21 miles from Burton Bradstock to Weymouth is extremely flat.

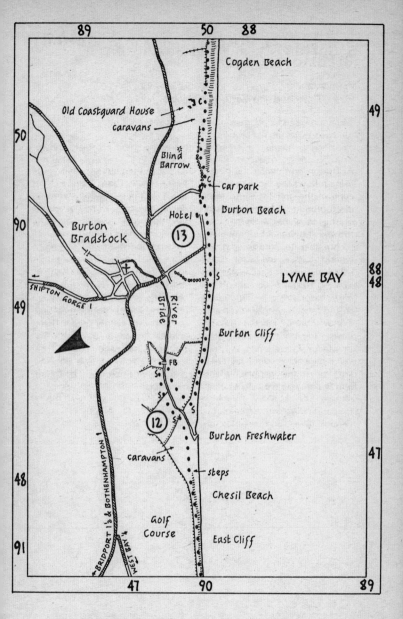

89   50   88

Cogden Beach

Old Coastguard House
caravans

49

Blind
Barrow

car park

Burton Beach

Hotel

Burton
Bradstock

13

SHIPTON GORGE 1

90

49

River Bride

88
48

LYME BAY

Burton Cliff

FB

12

Burton Freshwater

caravans

47

steps

Chesil Beach

48

Golf
Course

East Cliff

91

47   90   89

30
15   12   13

6. Burton Mere, West Bexington

2¼ miles
Maps: 1:25000 sheet SY58; 1:50000 sheet 194
Terrain: Dead level and mostly over shingle.

The official route passes inland of Burton Mere, but most wayfarers use the track on the seaward side. East of the Mere is a very uncomfortable stretch of the Path on loose shingle which continues as far as West Bexington.

Burton Mere is a sedge marsh, a refuge for wildfowl and an ornithologist's paradise.

Chesil Beach (Chesil is derived from the Saxon for shingle) is a huge natural barrier 18 miles long, 50 ft above sea level and 200 yds wide, erected by the power of the sea. It is said that knowledgeable mariners can tell where they are on the Beach in a mist, since the pebbles which form the shingle are very small at the western end – they are known as pea gravel – and gradually increase in size towards Portland. There have been many shipwrecks along this stretch of coast, and in November 1824 one 95-ton ship was blown over the beach into the Fleet.

Scenically, this is not an attractive section, although the prospect inland is pleasant enough. The hedges have been left behind and the drystone walls which form the field boundaries are covered with yellow lichen. There is much flotsam on the beach. On the marginal land behind the foreshore, sea kale, sea poppies and white campion will be found growing.

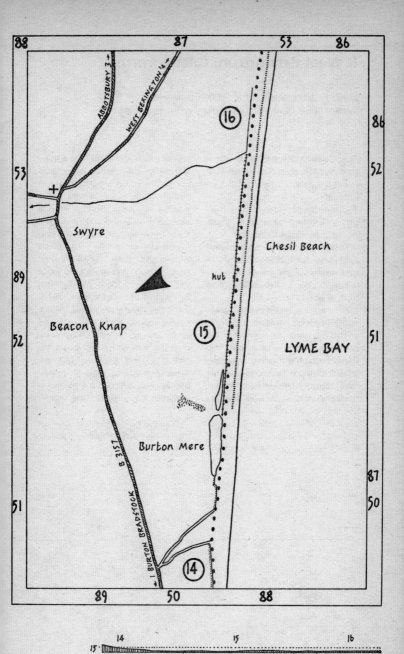

88 87 53 53 86

ABBOTSBURY 3
WEST BEXINGTON 14

16

86

53 52

+
Swyre

Chesil Beach

89

hut

Beacon Knap

15

52 51

LYME BAY

B 3157

Burton Mere

87

51 BURTON BRADSTOCK 50

14

89 50 88

14 15 16
15

7. West Bexington, Castle Farm

2½ miles
Maps: 1:25000 sheet SY58; 1:50000 sheet 194
Terrain: Still dead flat but the ground is firmer underfoot.

West Bexington has a grocer's shop, a café, a public house and a post office. Early closing is Tuesday.

There is a Youth Hostel at Litton Cheney, about 3 miles inland from West Bexington.

West-bound walkers will begin a 1½-mile stretch of uncomfortable walking on loose shingle between West Bexington and Burton Mere.

At West Bexington, east-bound walkers have to make the important decision whether to continue along the coast to Osmington Mills or to take the inland route via the Hardy monument and the Dorset Ridgeway.

The coastal route is absolutely flat and for most of the way follows the Fleet, a stretch of brackish water which lies on the inland side of Chesil Beach. The scenery is not particularly attractive but will appeal to those who like saltings and are interested in bird life. Abbotsbury is well worth visiting for the church, the tithe barn, St Catherine's Chapel, the Swannery and the sub-tropical gardens (see p. 44) but near Weymouth there is a 5-mile stretch which is completely urbanized. The distance between West Bexington and Osmington Mills, using the coastal route, is 23 miles.

The inland route is 16 miles long and is almost entirely on high ground, with fine views both inland and over the sea. There are many prehistoric remains which will appeal to those interested in archaeology. I prefer the inland route.

Those who decide to follow the inland diversion should now turn to p. 80.

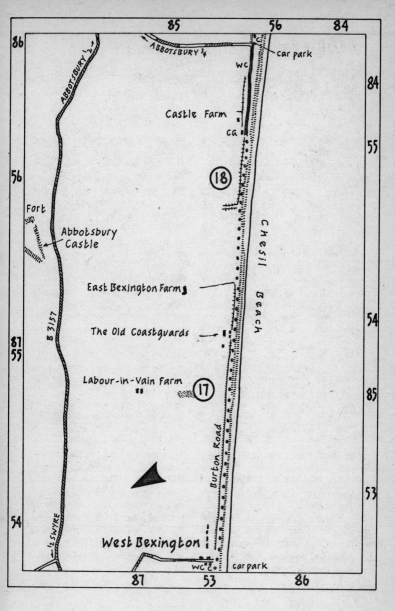

8. Abbotsbury, Walls Down

3½ miles
Maps: 1:25000 sheet SY58; 1:50000 sheet 194
Terrain: Still very flat, with 2 miles of road walking.

At mile 19, east-bound walkers must turn inland along the green lane to Abbotsbury in order to avoid the Swannery. Theoretically it is possible to walk along Chesil Beach as far as Portland, but this is *not recommended* – it is a desperately hard walk over 9 miles of shifting shingle. There is no way off the beach; wayfarers can only go on to Portland or retrace their steps. In rough weather it can be dangerous.

From Abbotsbury, those travelling west must take the un-metalled lane on the left-hand side of the road opposite 35A High Street.

East-bound walkers should take the road signposted 'New Barn and Swannery' and ignore the metalled lane signposted 'Footpath'. There are about 2 miles of road walking.

Abbotsbury has a grocer's shop, public house, a post office and accommodation. There is a bus service to Bridport and Weymouth. Early closing day is Thursday.

The parish church of St Nicholas is mainly Perpendicular and has a fine Jacobean pulpit and sounding board, a chancel with a seventeenth-century barrel ceiling and a west gallery. During restoration work done on the roof in 1930 two lead bullets were discovered, and certain marks on the pupit are reputed to be shot holes. It seems that fighting took place in the church, which the Royalists had garrisoned, when Abbotsbury was attacked by the Roundheads under Ashley-Cooper in 1644. The tithe barn to the south of the church is one of the finest examples in the whole country. It dates from the fifteenth century, measures 272 ft by 31 ft and contains an old threshing machine which was worked by a waterwheel.

The famous Swannery, now 400 years old, contains over 500 swans and a duck decoy. It is open daily from mid-May to mid-September. The sub-tropical gardens contain a collection of over 7,000 sub-tropical plants, including superb magnolias and camellias. They are open daily from mid-March to October.

St Catherine's Chapel, situated on a prominent hill, was probably built as a landmark for mariners. It contains a unique stone ceiling and is worth visiting for the view over the surrounding countryside.

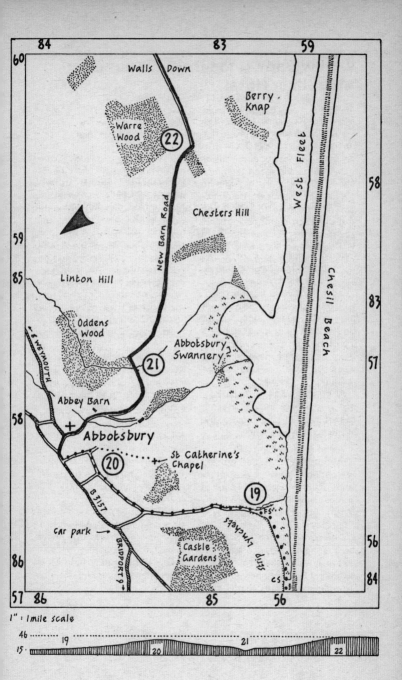

9. New Barn, Rodden Hive, Herbury, Moonfleet Hotel

3¼ miles
Maps: 1:25000 sheet SY68/78; 1:50000 sheet 194
Terrain: From New Barn Farm the path crosses fields and then runs along the edge of the Fleet.

There are long-term plans to provide a path inland of the road. Until this happy day dawns it is necessary for eastbound walkers to go through the farmyard at New Barn Farm to reach a muddy, enclosed lane. At Bridge Lane Farm the Coastal Path is rejoined by a Coast Path sign.

Until the diversion is provided, west-bound walkers must ignore the north-facing signpost at Bridge Lane Farm and keep to the left of the farm. On reaching New Barn Farm they have about 2 miles of road walking before reaching Abbotsbury.

At point A, walkers must take to the foreshore for a few yards to skirt the hedge. Ignore the stile in the barbed-wire fence.

Langton Herring, a mile inland, gets its odd name from the Harangs or Herings who were Lords of the Manor in the Middle Ages. It is an attractive village well screened by trees, with a delightful sixteenth-century public house and restaurant, the Elm Tree, which serves excellent meals and bar snacks.

The name 'Hive', which occurs frequently along this stretch of coast, is old English for 'landing place'.

The Path now follows the Fleet, a stretch of brackish water enclosed by Chesil Beach, as far as Weymouth. It is the haunt of wildfowl, swans and fishermen.

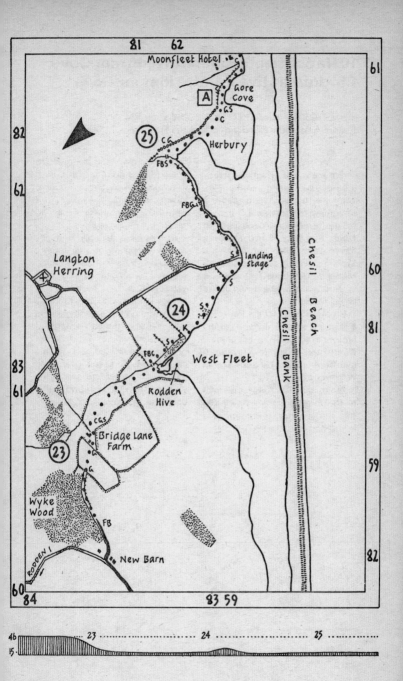

10. Moonfleet Hotel, Butterstreet Cove, Chickerell Hive Point, Tidmoor Cove

3½ miles
Maps: 1:25000 sheet SY67/77; 1:50000 sheet 194
Terrain: A flat route along the edge of the Fleet.

The Moonfleet Hotel has accommodation and serves meals. It figures prominently in that stirring tale of eighteenth-century smuggling, *Moonfleet*, by J. Meade Faulkner (published in 1898). The Why Not? bar gets its name from the arms of the Mohune family (corrupted to Moon in Moonfleet) which is a cross pall on a shield and looks like a Y-knot.

Chickerell, just off the Path, has a grocer's shop, a café, a public house, a post office, accommodation and buses to Weymouth and Bridport. Early closing day is Wednesday.

When the rifle range between miles 28 and 29 is in use, red flags are flown and sentries are posted at both ends of the Path to escort walkers over the range. *When the red flag is flying do not cross the range without an escort.*

At East Fleet are a few cottages and the remains of the church. The village was inundated by the sea and destroyed by the great gale of 1824. In the church can be seen brasses to the Mohune family and underneath the floor is their vault in which contraband was stored. There was a secret passage which led out to the churchyard. This, too, was used as a setting for *Moonfleet* – the youthful hero was trapped with a corpse in the vault.

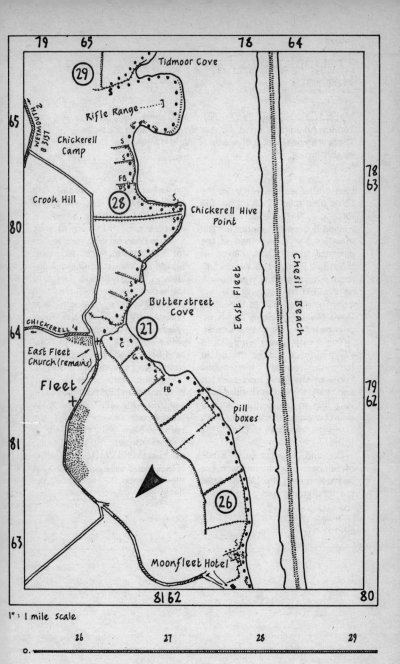

79 65   78   64

② 29   Tidmoor Cove

65   Rifle Range·······]

WEYMOUTH 2 B 3157

Chickerell
Camp   78
                                        63
Crook Hill   S
                        S
                     FB
              28   DS
                        S
                     Chickerell Hive
                             Point
80   S

                         S
                    S
                  S
            Butterstreet
               Cove

CHICKERELL 'a   27   East Fleet
64   Chesil Beach
East Fleet   C
Church (remains)   G
                                        79
Fleet   S   62
    +   FB
                           pill
                           boxes

81

26

63   S

            Moonfleet Hotel

              81 62   80

1" : 1 mile scale

        26   27   28   29

o.

49

11. Linch Cove, Ferrybridge, Portland Harbour

3½ miles
Maps: 1:25000 sheet SY67/77; 1:50000 sheet 194
Terrain: An uninspiring section somewhat urban in character.
There is an unpleasant diversion to avoid a Ministry of Defence establishment.

East-bound walkers will leave the fields near mile 32 to follow the foreshore. If the exact point is missed it does not matter, as the main road will be joined at the entrance to a holiday camp. At the A354 Portland to Weymouth road, 4 miles of road walking can be avoided by catching the bus from Derwent Road to Bowleaze Cove (mile 37). Some buses go only as far as Overcombe Corner.

The most direct route into Weymouth is to take the urban footpath opposite the public house on the A354 road, turn left and walk along the disused railway line to the cutting. At this point bear right to follow the Path along the foreshore to Old Castle Road.

Portland, Thomas Hardy's Isle of Slingers (he chose the name because during the Middle Ages the inhabitants had a reputation for being good sling shots), is a peninsula which is joined to the mainland by Chesil Beach. It consists almost entirely of rock and has been extensively quarried for building material. Some of London's finest buildings, including Whitehall and St Paul's Cathedral, are constructed from Portland stone, which was brought by ship up the River Thames. For a long time there was a convict settlement in Portland Bill, but the prison buildings have been converted to a Borstal.

Portland harbour is a naval base and warships are often to be seen riding at anchor. The huge breakwaters which protect the harbour were built to defend it against torpedo attack. During the First World War the battleship H M S *Hood* was scuttled across the entrance to reinforce the defences.

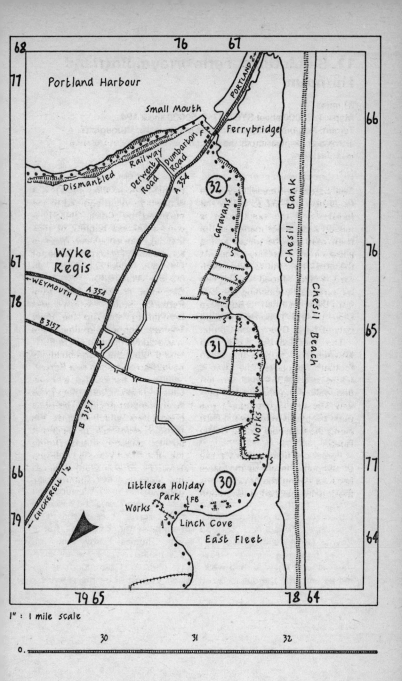

I" : I mile scale

12. Sandsfoot Castle, Weymouth, Lodmoor

3 miles
Maps: 1 : 25000 sheet SY67/77; 1 : 50000 sheet 194
Terrain: Flat, urban and scenically uninteresting, although there are pleasant views across the harbour.

East-bound walkers in a hurry to reach Weymouth can reach the centre of the town by following Rodwell Road.

Sandsfoot Castle was built by Henry VIII in 1539 as part of a chain of forts to protect the principal harbours of the south coast. Two miles away across the harbour is Portland Castle, so that any attack from the sea was subject to cross-fire. Much of the ramparts and gun emplacements have succumbed to the relentless attack of nature and have fallen into the sea. The castle is now owned by the Corporation and has been laid out with pleasant gardens.

Weymouth has shops, cafés, restaurants, public houses, banks, a post office, accommodation and train and bus services to Bristol and London. There are bus services to Abbotsbury, Axminster, Bournemouth, Bowleaze Cove, Bridport, Dorchester, Littlemoor, Osmington Mills, Preston, Salisbury, Sutton Poyntz, Upwey and Wool.

East-bound walkers can save themselves 2 miles of road walking by catching the bus to Bowleaze Cove or Overcombe Corner.

Although having a population of over 40,000 there is little in Weymouth which is memorable. It is a pleasant enough town, except for the western end, which is vulgar and trippery. A stroll round the old shopping centre will reveal some pleasant townscapes, with narrow alleys and some bow-fronted houses with iron balconies. Around the quayside are some attractive old buildings.

During the eighteenth century Weymouth was a fashionable watering place and was one of George III's favourite resorts. Fanny Burney came here in 1789 with Queen Charlotte and describes how the King entered the water in a bathing machine: 'A machine follows the royal one into the sea, filled with fiddlers, who play "God save the King" as his Majesty takes the plunge.' Jane Austen used Weymouth in a scene from *Emma* and describes the town as 'one of the idlest haunts in the kingdom'. But it was Thomas Hardy who put Weymouth on the literary map. Re-christened Budmouth, it figures in most of his major novels.

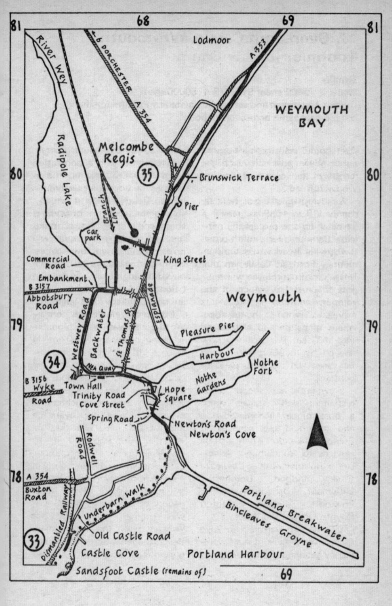

81 **68** **69** **81**

River Wey

Lodmoor

A 353

A 6 DORCHESTER

A 354

WEYMOUTH
BAY

Radipole Lake

Melcombe
Regis

35

Branch Line

car
park

Brunswick Terrace

80 **80**

Pier

Commercial
Road

King Street

Embankment

B 3157
Abbotsbury
Road

Westway Road

Backwater

St Thomas St.

Esplanade

Weymouth

79 **79**

Pleasure Pier

34

NEW Quay

Harbour

Nothe
Fort

B 315b
Wyke
Road

Town Hall
Trinity Road
Cove street

Hope
Square

Nothe
Gardens

Spring Road

Newton's Road
Newton's Cove

Rodwell Road

78 Portland Breakwater **78**

A 354
Buxton
Road

Dismantled Railway

Underbarn Walk

Bincleaves Groyne

33

Old Castle Road

Castle Cove

Portland Harbour

Sandsfoot Castle (remains of)

69

15   33   34   35

13. Overcombe, Bowleaze Cove, Pontin's Holiday Camp

2½ miles
Maps: 1:25000 sheet SY68/78; 1:50000 sheet 194
Terrain: An unattractive section dominated by Pontin's huge hotel. It gets better once past the hotel.

Overcombe has a grocer's shop, public house, post office, accommodation and a bus service to Weymouth.

Westward-travelling walkers can avoid 4 miles of road walking by catching the bus from Bowleaze Cove or Overcombe Corner to Derwent Road, at Ferrybridge on the western side of Weymouth (mile 32). If you crave the fleshpots of Weymouth you can break your journey there.

Just to the north of the road which forms part of the Coast Path are the remains of a small Roman temple. It is sited on the top of Jordan Hill and must have been visible from miles away.

From Redcliff Point it is possible to see the figure of George III cut in the chalk above Sutton Poyntz. It is a huge figure depicting him riding away from Weymouth and measures 280 ft long and 323 ft high.

Sutton Poyntz is Hardy's Overcombe, the village in which many of the main events of *The Trumpet-Major* are set.

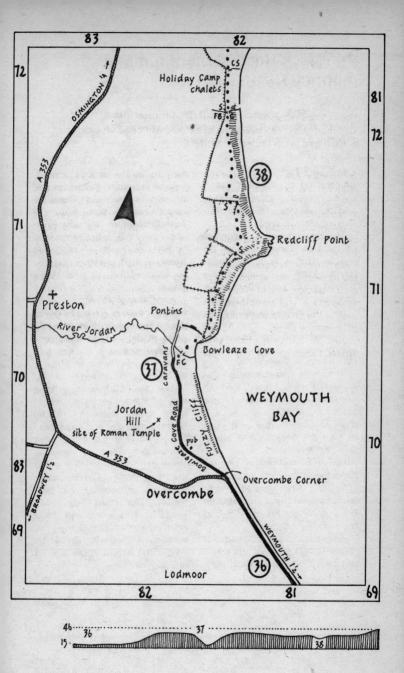

83

82

72

OSMINGTON ¼

A 353

Holiday Camp
chalets

CS

S
FB

72

81

72

71

38

S

Redcliff Point

71

Preston

River Jordan

Pontins

71

Caravans

Bowleaze Cove

37

FC

WEYMOUTH
BAY

70

Jordan
Hill
site of Roman Temple

Cove Road

Furzy Cliff

83

A 353

BROADWEY 1½

Bowleaze

pub

Overcombe Corner

69

Overcombe

WEYMOUTH 1½

70

36

Lodmoor

82

81

69

46

36

37

15

38

55

14. Black Head, Osmington Mills, Burning Cliff

2½ miles
Maps: 1:25000 sheet SY68/78; 1:50000 sheet 194
Terrain: Those travelling eastwards will find this section very pleasant compared with the last few miles.

Osmington Mills has a seasonal grocer's on the caravan site, a public house, accommodation and bus services to Weymouth, Osmington and Wool.

The Smugglers Inn, which lies on the Path, serves delicious bar snacks. The notorious smuggler 'French Peter' is reputed to have plotted with the landlord while an exciseman hid in the chimney.

Osmington has a grocer's shop, café, public house, post office, accommodation and bus services to Weymouth and Wool. Early closing day is Wednesday.

At Fisher's Piece between miles 40 and 41 the true line of the Path runs through the gardens on the seaward side of the houses. It is more polite and easier on the feet to take the track on the inland side of the houses.

Lobsters are caught on the rocks below the cliffs hereabouts.

Burning Cliff gets its name because the oil shales of which it is made caught fire in 1826 and burnt for a year.

Ringstead is a medieval deserted village lying just south of Glebe Cottage. It is still pos-sible to see the layout of the village by examining the bumps and hollows in the grass. There are two theories to account for the abandonment of the settlement: one that the inhabitants fled before the French in 1420 and never returned; the other that they were killed off by the Black Death.

At Osmington Mills, west-bound walkers will have to decide whether to follow the 23 miles of flat and scenically un-attractive coastline (including 5 miles around Weymouth which is completely urbanized) or to follow the 16-mile high-level inland alternative. The inland route follows the line of the Dorset Ridgeway and has splen-did views over the sea. It has numerous prehistoric remains along its route which will excite the imagination of those inter-ested in archaeology and pre-history. The coast route will appeal to bird lovers and those who like the atmosphere of marshes. Those who decide to follow the inland route should turn to p. 90.

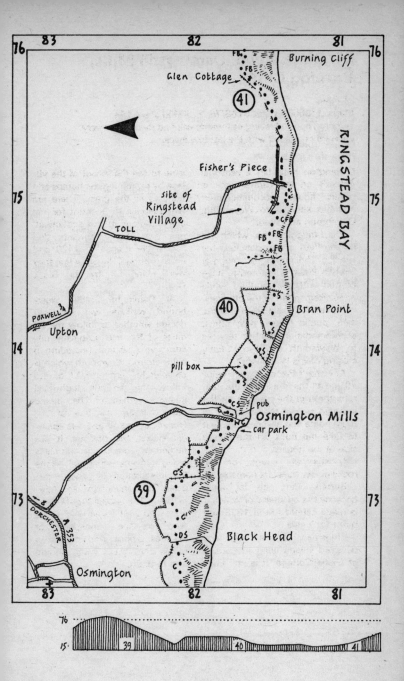

15. Ringstead Bay, White Nothe, Bat's Head

2¾ miles
Maps: 1:25000 sheets SY68/78 and SY69/79; 1:50000
sheet 194
Terrain: Splendid cliff walk for most of the way.
There are superb views.

East-bound walkers must be sure to cross the stile by the Coast Path signpost next to the chapel.

The obelisk is a marker for shipping.

The turf on this section of the Path is splendidly springy, and if the weather is fine the walker will stride along joyfully revelling in the magnificent coastal scenery.

Once on to the cliffs, few people are likely to be encountered before reaching Durdle Door. White Nothe is the first chalk cliff to be met by those travelling eastward and it is the herald of the finest section of the whole path. From now until reaching the Foreland, almost at journey's end, the great whale-backs of the Downs end abruptly at the edge of the sea. From now on the flora changes to a chalk habitat and we can look for scabious and bee orchids. Note, too, the attractive stratification of the cliffs which have been twisted and torn by the movement of the earth. At Bat's Head the strata is vertical.

The Warren is the remains of an old Celtic field system.

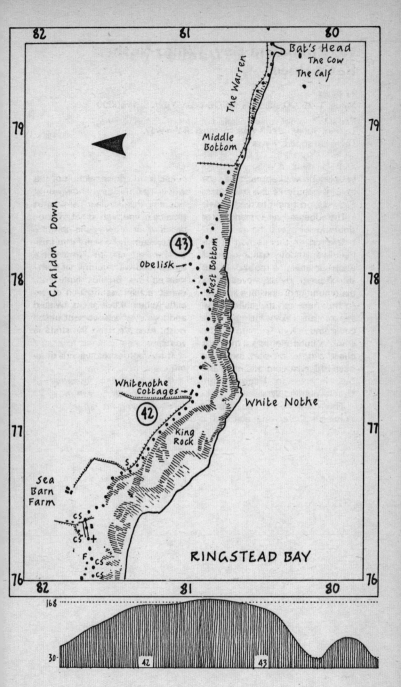

16. Swyre Head, Durdle Door, Lulworth Cove

2½ miles
Maps: 1 : 25000 sheet SY88/98; 1 : 50000 sheet 194
Terrain: Another superb section of strenuous cliff walking.

Durdle Door, with its natural sea arch, is a famous beauty spot. All walkers will appreciate the natural beauty of this stretch of Path, but it is those with some knowledge and understanding of geology who will be most appreciative.

Lulworth Cove has a grocer's shop, a café, a public house which serves meals, a post office, accommodation and bus services to Bournemouth, Dorchester and Weymouth. Early closing day is Saturday.

West Lulworth has a grocer's shop, a café, a public house, a post office, accommodation and bus services to Bournemouth, Dorchester and Weymouth.

There are two routes around Lulworth Cove, one across the beach and the other over the cliffs.

Eastward-travelling walkers will enter the firing ranges at Fossil Forest Gate. They must time their arrival at the range when it is open (see p. 11), otherwise they will be faced with a 12-mile walk to Kimmeridge along roads. The army has way-marked the 6-mile route with posts placed at 100-yd intervals. About 70,000 shells are fired each year which necessitates a detail searching the Path before the ranges are opened to ensure that no high-explosive shells are left.

It is absolutely essential to observe the rules given on p. 11 while crossing the range.

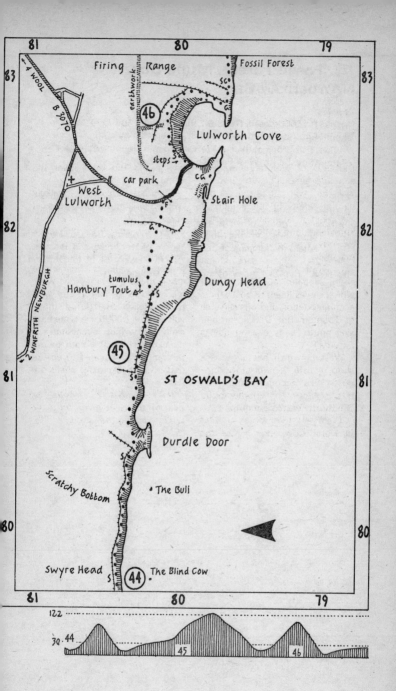

17. Fossil Forest, Mupe Bay, Worbarrow Bay

3 miles
Maps: 1:25000 sheets SY88/98 and SY87/97; 1:50000
sheet 194
Terrain: This is one of the most rewarding and arduous sections
of the whole South-West Peninsular Coast Path.

After entering the firing ranges by the Bindon Gate, some steps will be observed going down to the sea. These lead to the fossil forest, where the remains of trees some 200 million years old may be seen. Fern-like trees of this kind once covered the whole of the country and were the habitat of dinosaurs.

At Worbarrow Bay may be seen some of the finest and most attractive examples of folding and cliff stratification.

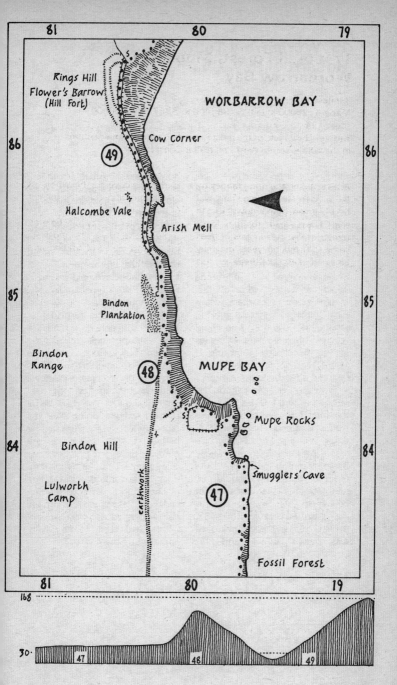

WORBARROW BAY

Rings Hill
Flower's Barrow
(Hill Fort)

Cow Corner

⑭⑨

Halcombe Vale

Arish Mell

Bindon
Plantation

Bindon
Range

⑭⑧

MUPE BAY

Bindon Hill

Mupe Rocks

Lulworth
Camp

earthwork

Smugglers' Cave

⑭⑦

Fossil Forest

168

30·   47   48   49

18. Worbarrow Tout, Brandy Bay, Hobarrow Bay, Charnel

2½ miles
Maps: 1:25000 sheets SY88/98 and SY87/97; 1:50000 sheets 194 and 195
Terrain: Another splendid section, this time with some good inland views.

From Warbarrow Tout there are splendid views of the coast. Tout is an old English word meaning lookout. Tyneham Cap is 550 ft high, but because the top is tilted inward there are no views.

Eastward of Tyneham Cap the chalk gives way to Kimmeridge Shale, an almost black, oily stone which can be worked on a lathe. In prehistoric times there was a local industry based on making ornaments and household articles. There are good examples in the Dorchester Museum. It seems that nothing was manufactured after the fourth century.

Tyneham village cannot be reached from the Coast Path, but the inland road is open during August and occasionally at other times. The village and Elizabethan manor house were taken over by the army during the war with the promise that they would be returned after the cessation of hostilities; that promise still remains to be honoured. In 1967, the east front of the Manor House was taken down and re-constructed at Athelhampton. It is sad that such a beautiful house should have been so wantonly destroyed.

By one of those curious ironies, the army, which does not allow general access to the firing ranges, has preserved much of the prehistoric and medieval heritage of the Tyneham valley. Throughout Dorset many barrows, old settlements, field systems and ancient boundaries have disappeared under the plough, but although peppered with unexploded shells there remain three complete medieval field systems, an Iron Age field system, and here and there traces of medieval ploughing over the older cultivation. Because neither herbicides nor pesticides are normally used in the ranges there is a great wealth of fauna and flora. Indeed it is one of the few places left in England with a rich variety of wild flowers. The birds have adjusted to their violent habitat and seem to be totally unmoved by the firing.

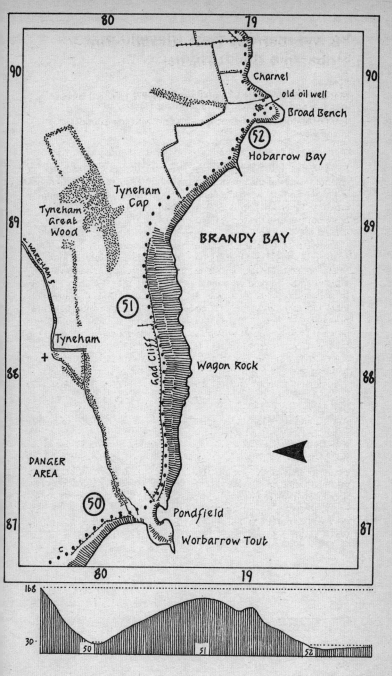

19. Kimmeridge Bay, Clavell's Hard, Rope Lake Head, Eldon Seat

3 miles
Maps: 1:25000 sheet SY87/97; 1:50000 sheet 195
Terrain: Good cliff walking with some steep climbs and splendid views.

Kimmeridge has a grocer's shop, a café, a post office and accommodation. Early closing day is Thursday.

West-bound walkers will enter the army's firing ranges at Kimmeridge Gate. They must time their arrival at the range when it is open (see p. 11) to avoid a 12-mile walk to Lulworth Cove along roads.

The 6-mile route has been waymarked by the army. White posts are to be found at 100-yd intervals so there is no excuse for straying from the Path. An army detail searches the Path before it is opened to ensure that none of the 70,000 high-explosive, armour-piercing shells which are fired each year has failed to explode and is lying near the Path.

It is absolutely essential to observe the rules given on p. 11 while crossing the range.

Kimmeridge has some 'nodding donkey' oil wells, part of British Petroleum's exploration of the Kimmeridge shale.

The Clavell Tower, near mile 53, was built in 1820 by the Reverend John Clavell, of Smedmore. Its purpose is not known for certain, some authorities maintaining that it is a folly, others that it was used as an observatory. Incorporated into the structure is a scholarly mixture of classical motifs, which together with the Tuscan columns and false machicolation favour the folly theory, but the parapet would serve very well to support a small astronomical telescope.

Smedmore House, which is open to the public during the summer, lies about a mile off the Path and to the east of Kimmeridge. It was built by Sir William Clavell in 1632 and was altered and extended in the eighteenth century. Sir William was something of a failed industrialist. He boiled seawater to extract the salt, using the Kimmeridge shale as a fuel. He then established an alum factory in defiance of the monopoly granted by Charles I to certain London merchants. Later he tried to turn Kimmeridge into a port by constructing a stone jetty, but this, too, failed.

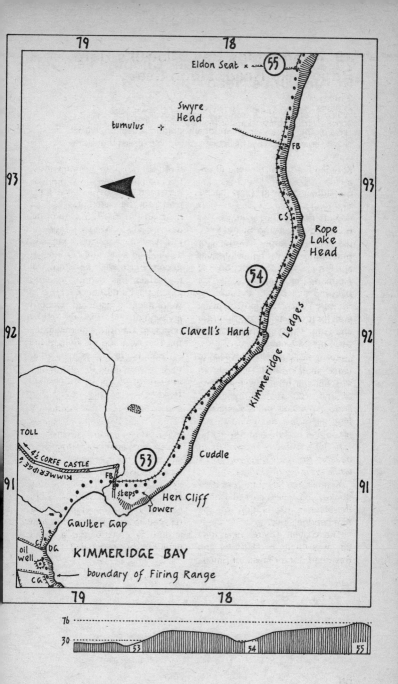

KIMMERIDGE BAY

boundary of Firing Range

20. Encombe Waterfall, Chapman's Pool, St Aldhelm's Head

3 miles
Maps: 1:25000 sheet SY87/97; 1:50000 sheet 195
Terrain: This is another exceptionally strenuous section, with hills so steep that steps have been provided to assist the weary walker.

St Aldhelm's Head (also called St Alban's Head) is 350 ft high and offers magnificent views. The chapel, dedicated to St Aldhelm, the eighth-century Bishop of Sherborne, has the typically squat and massive construction of Norman architecture. It is believed that one of the reasons for siting it at this remote place was for it to serve as a marker for shipping. The centre turret might have held a lantern.

From St Aldhelm's Head to Swanage there is much evidence of quarrying for Purbeck stone.

Encombe House, some way inland from the waterfall, was built by John Pitt in 1735. One of his descendants, William Moreton Pitt, was a prison reformer and established a sail and cord mill at Encombe. He went bankrupt and the estate was bought by Lord Eldon, the Lord Chancellor. Eldon was a splendid rearguard reactionary who distinguished himself by opposing Catholic emancipation, the Test Acts and the Reform Bill of 1832. His last speech in Parliament was against the dangerous innovation of the Great Western Railway.

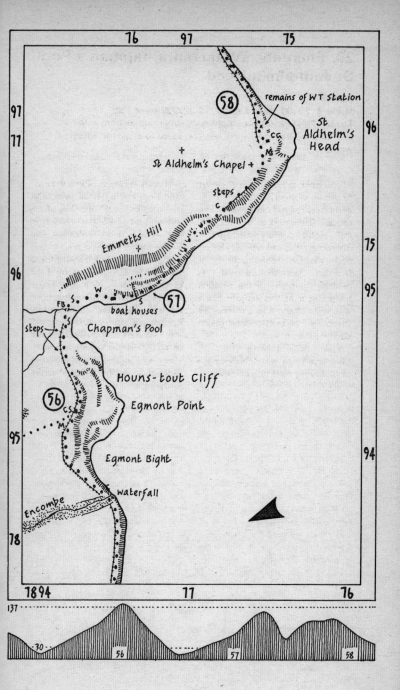

remains of WT Station

58

St Aldhelm's Head

CG

MS

+ St Aldhelm's Chapel +

steps

C

Emmetts Hill

W

FB S

S

57

boat houses

Chapman's Pool

steps

Houns-tout Cliff

56

CS

Egmont Point

M

Egmont Bight

waterfall

Encombe

137

30

56

57

58

21. West Man, Seacombe Cliff, Dancing Ledge

3 miles
Maps: 1:25000 sheet SY87/97; 1:50000 sheet 195
Terrain: Splendid cliff-top walking.

There are some fine examples of strip lynchets – platforms cut into the hillside for agricultural purposes – on either side of mile 59. At one time archaeologists thought that they were of Iron Age origin and were used because they provided good drainage. However, it is now generally accepted that these terraces would not have provided very good crops and it is believed that they are of Saxon origin and result from land hunger. As the best soil was all under the plough and still could not supply the population with all the food that they needed, it was necessary to employ such methods to prevent starvation. There is now much interest in ancient farming methods and the experimental farm at Butser Hill in Hampshire is trying to re-create Iron Age methods of cultivation. Our ancient British forbears were very good farmers and I know of one Dorset farmer who was so impressed with the prehistoric drainage system he found on his land that he connected his own field drainage system to it and then applied for an agricultural drainage grant. He caused consternation among local officials!

At East Man are the graves of the 168 passengers lost when the East Indian *Halsewell* was wrecked in 1786. Heroic efforts were made by local people but only 80 were saved.

From Dancing Ledge, stones from the quarries were loaded on to ships. There is a swimming pool cut into the rock.

Worth Matravers, a mile inland, is an exceptionally beautiful village. The church of St Nicholas of Myra is mostly Norman. Apart from its intrinsic architectural interest it is also noteworthy for containing the grave of Benjamin Jesty, who, according to his epitaph, '... was born at Yetminster in this county and was an upright and honest man, particularly modest for being the first Person known that introduced the Cow Pox by inoculation and who from his great strength of mind made the Experiment from the Cow on his Wife and two Sons'. Apparently, he used the technique of inoculation 20 years before Jenner.

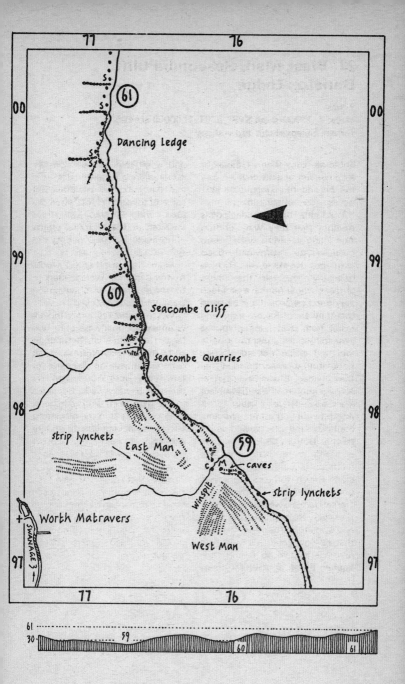

22. Blacker's Hole, Anvil Point, Durlston Head

3 miles
Maps: 1:25000 sheet SY97/SZ07; 1:50000 sheet 195
Terrain: Easy walking on good paths.

Between miles 61 and 63 there are a number of parallel paths, but walkers cannot go wrong providing they do not stray inland.

The lighthouse on Anvil Point, which may be visited on most afternoons, is a Mountain Rescue Post! This was established, not so much as a tribute to the glorious hills of Dorset, as for the benefit of the many climbers who practise their sport on the sea cliffs hereabouts.

The tall posts are shipping markers originally used to establish the maximum speed of warships during their speed trials. They are exactly one nautical mile apart, and there is a duplicate set some way inland. By using a stop watch and lining up the two sets of markers the exact speed could be calculated.

Tilly Whim caves are the remains of an old quarry. The curious name is derived from the name of the owner, Mr Tilly, who used a whim (or crane) to extract the stone and lower it into boats.

The great globe of Portland stone on Durlston Head is 10 ft in diameter and weighs 40 tons. It was given by George Burt, a Swanage stone merchant, who built the Durlston Castle Restaurant on the cliff top. It was designed in the 1890s in the heyday of British imperial power and it makes an interesting test of general knowledge to discover how many Third World countries can now be identified.

The path from Durlston Head to Swanage is not very interesting and is much frequented by local strollers.

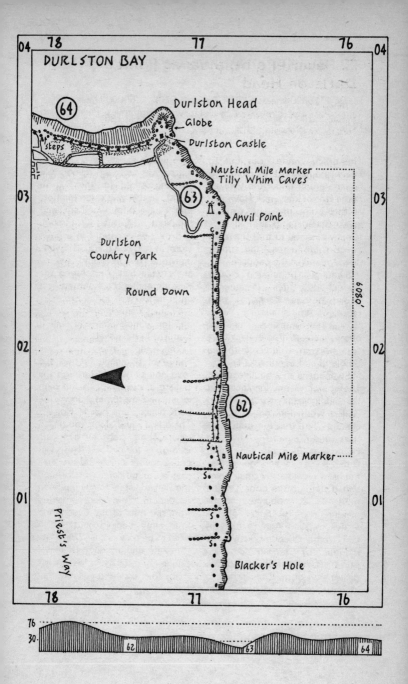

DURLSTON BAY

64

Durlston Head

Globe

Durlston Castle

Nautical Mile Marker

Tilly Whim Caves

63

Anvil Point

Durlston
Country Park

Round Down

62

Nautical Mile Marker

steps

6080'

Priest's Way

Blacker's Hole

76

30

62

63

64

23. Peveril Point, Swanage, Ballard Point

4 miles
Maps: 1:25000 sheets SY97/SZ07 and SZ08; 1:50000 sheet 195
Terrain: A dull stretch of walking which improves near Ballard Point.

The official route goes out to Peveril Point and then along the foreshore and under the terraces of the Hotel Grosvenor. However, at this point the Path can be awash at certain tides. Most wayfarers will prefer to take the more direct route across the grassy down inland of the car park.

Swanage (population 8,000) has shops, cafés, restaurants, public houses, banks, a post office, accommodation, a Youth Hostel and campsites. There are bus services to Poole via Wareham and to Bournemouth via Studland and Sandbanks Ferry.

Swanage is an attractive resort. The church is unremarkable but the old lock-up near the Town Hall is worth looking at. It was erected 'For the Prevention of Vice and Immorality by the Friends of Religion and Good Order, A D 1803' and the ventilation was provided by small holes drilled through the door. On the front is a monument commemorating the defeat of the Danes by King Alfred's navy in 887, rather incongruously surmounted by Crimean War cannon balls. A brief account of the destruction of the Danish fleet is given in The Anglo-Saxon Chronicle, which seems to show that nature was as much responsible as King Alfred for the Danish plight: 'In this year came the host into Exeter from Wareham, and the pirate host sailed west about, and they were caught in a great storm at sea, and there off Swanage one hundred and twenty ships were lost. And Alfred the King rode after the mounted host with his levies as far as Exeter.'

Thomas Hardy lodged in Swanage for a short time and calls it Knollsea in his novels.

The official route from the centre of Swanage follows the road and turns east through the Ballard estate. The cliff-top path is reached by turning down the path which runs beside No. 22. There is a route along the beach where some steps by a stream lead up to the cliff top. However, connoisseurs of the bizarre may prefer the offical route through the Ballard estate to see the bijou residences cunningly converted from the huts of the First World War army encampment which used to be on this site. The estate is private, and although there is a public right of way for pedestrians the estate roads are not open to unauthorized traffic.

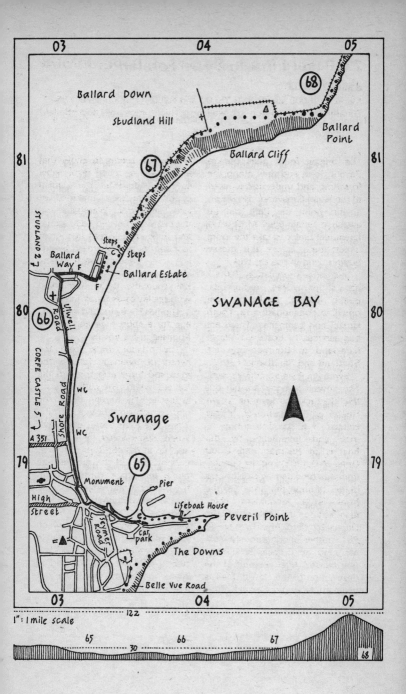

03   04   05

Ballard Down

Studland Hill

68

Ballard Point

67

Ballard Cliff

81

Studland 2

Ballard Way

F

C

steps

steps

Ballard Estate

F

F

SWANAGE BAY

66

Ullwell Road

80

CORFE CASTLE 5

Shore Road

WC

WC

Swanage

A 351

79

65

Monument

Pier

High Street

Eymer Road

Lifeboat House

Peveril Point

Car Park

The Downs

Belle Vue Road

03   04   05

122

1": 1 mile scale

65   66   67

30   68

24. The Pinnacles, The Foreland, Studland

2½ miles
Maps: 1:25000 sheet SZ08; 1:50000 sheet 195
Terrain: An interesting cliff-top walk.

The Foreland is a magnificent vantage point, with the sea boiling round the twin stacks of Old Harry and Old Harry's Wife.

This is the last viewpoint for east-bound walkers, for the rest of the route is dull and flat. If the mood is right, take off your rucksack, sit and admire the view, muse on the experiences of the walk and thank whatever gods you acknowledge for the beauty of Britain and the gifts of health and strength which have allowed you to enjoy it. Spare a thought, too, for all those who have laboured to provide such a magnificent walk. Walkers who have come the whole distance from Minehead have well over 600 miles under their boots and countless thousands of feet of climbing. But much more important than the mere pride of physical achievement is the spiritual refreshment gained from drinking so deeply at the wells of natural beauty.

Walkers travelling west will, from the Foreland, be able to savour some of the delights which lie ahead.

Studland has a grocer's shop, a café, a public house, accommodation and buses to Swanage and Bournemouth (via the Sandbanks Ferry). The parish church of St Nicholas of Myra, the patron saint of sailors, is one of the best examples of a Norman church in the whole country. In the churchyard is the grave of Sergeant William Lawrence of the 40th Regiment of Foot, who fought in the Peninsular War and at Waterloo. With his French wife Clothilde, he ran a public house until his death in 1869. He dictated his autobiography to a friend and it makes very interesting reading.

From Studland, the Path goes down to the beach near the car park and follows the foreshore along firm sand to the end of the Path at Shell Bay.

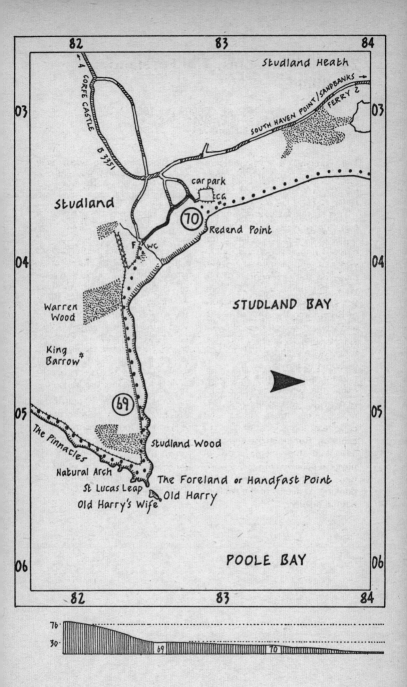

Studland Heath

CORFE CASTLE

B 3351

SOUTH HAVEN POINT / SANDBANKS

FERRY 2

Studland

car park
c.G.

70

Redend Point

F   wc

Warren
Wood

King
Barrow

STUDLAND BAY

69

The Pinnacles

Studland Wood

Natural Arch

St Lucas Leap

The Foreland or Handfast Point

Old Harry

Old Harry's Wife

POOLE BAY

76
30

69   70

25. Studland Bay, Shell Bay, Sandbanks Ferry

2 miles
Maps: 1:25000 sheet SZ07; 1:50000 sheet 195
Terrain: A level walk along sand dunes or the firm sand by the sea edge.

The Path follows the undulating dunes and heathland bordering the beach, but except on windy days when the sand is blowing it is easier to walk along the fine, firm sand of the beach.

Just behind the sand dunes is the Studland Heath National Nature Reserve, which can be reached from Knoll House, about a mile outside Studland on the road to South Haven Point. It is one of the last remaining pieces of primitive heathland, as described by Thomas Hardy, and is the habitat of the smooth snake and the sand lizard as well as rare plants and birds. A nature trail leaflet can be obtained at the Reserve or by writing to: National Nature Conservancy Council, South West Region, Roughmoor, Bishop's Hall, Taunton, Somerset TA1 5AA.

South Haven Point is the end (or the beginning!) of the South West Way. From here there is a frequent bus service to Swanage and Bournemouth.

A chain ferry to Sandbanks operates every 20 minutes from early in the morning until late at night.

Bournemouth, with a population of 150,000, has all the facilities of a large town and has excellent train and express coach services to London, the Midlands and the North, Weymouth, Portsmouth and the South Coast.

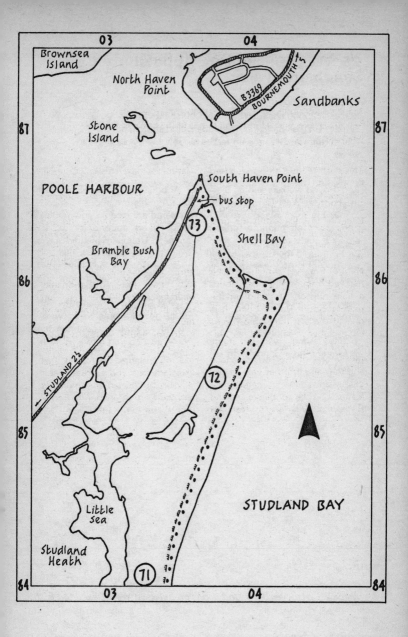

26. West Bexington, Abbotsbury Castle, Wears Hill

2¾ miles
Maps: 1:25000 sheet SY58; 1:50000 sheet 194
Terrain: On the whole, this is an unexciting stretch, but on Wears Hill, which is now under the plough, there are extensive views.

East-bound walkers should leave the coast at West Bexington and follow the road inland. Where it turns sharp left, continue forward along a track to the main road, turn right and then enter the field on the right. At the end of this field the ground is broken and overgrown, with no clear path. However, walkers will not go far wrong if they aim diagonally for the road.

West-bound walkers should experience little difficulty in following the route.

Abbotsbury Castle is a bivallate Iron Age hill fort and, as the path runs under the banks and ditches, there is an opportunity to examine it. There are splendid views from the top and it is believed that the Romans may have used the site to construct a signalling station.

West Bexington marks the end of the inland alternative for west-bound walkers. To continue the route they should now turn to p. 42.

West Bexington marks the end of the inland alternative for west-bound walkers. To continue the route they should now turn to p. 42.

Maps 26–31 cover the inland diversion between West Bexington and Osmington Mills.

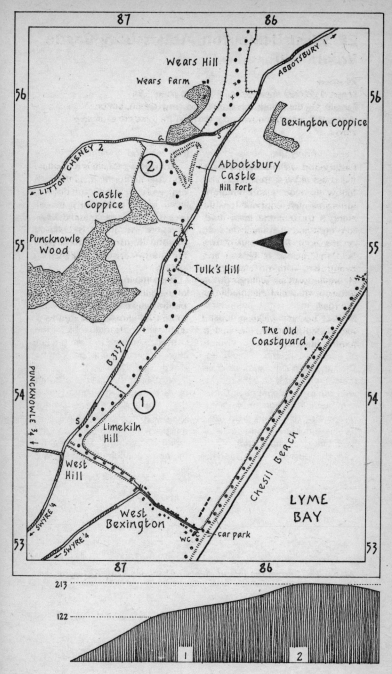

27. Wears Hill, White Hill, Bishop's Road, Portesham Road

2½ miles
Maps: 1:25000 sheet SY58; 1:50000 sheet 194
Terrain: Excellent high-level walking with extensive views
seaward.

There are splendid views to the south across Abbotsbury, which is laid out like a map, to the sea.

It is fascinating to note how strong are the influences of the Iron Age and medieval periods on this landscape. On the hills near the sea can be seen fine examples of Saxon strip lynchets (see p. 70) together with numerous tumuli and old enclosures. But it is the church which has made the strongest mark. Just before the Norman Conquest, Orc, a house-carl of King Canute, founded a Benedictine monastery which prospered until the Dissolution. The tithe barn still exists, as does the church, and it was the monks who built the Chapel of St Catherine which stands prominently on the little hill. It has been used for centuries by mariners as a landmark to aid navigation.

In the postwar years modern fertilizers and government grants have made it profitable to plough the downland which had lain undisturbed since prehistoric times. Sheep which have grazed here for countless centuries have now given way to cereals and this traditionally open landscape has been enclosed by ugly wire fences.

The route in the large field near mile 4 is indistinct on the ground. Walkers travelling east should keep roughly parallel to the wood on the left and should look for the farm road coming in from the left after passing the edge of the wood.

West-bound walkers should leave Bishop's Road and follow the farm road until it swings sharply to the right. Leave it at this point and walk parallel to the wood on the right until meeting the fence coming in from the left.

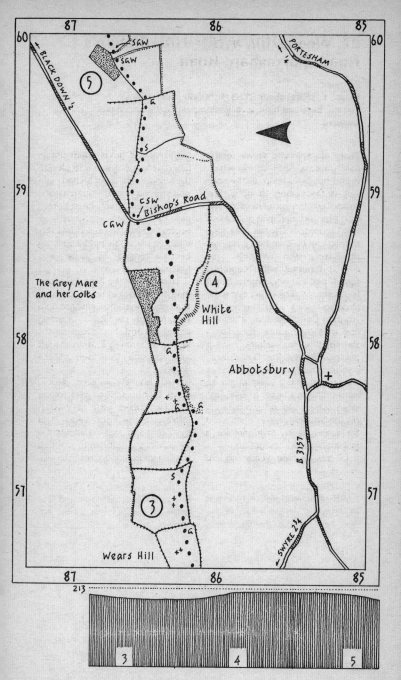

28. Portesham Road, The Hardy Monument, Corton Down

3 miles
Maps: 1:25000 sheet SY68/78; 1:50000 sheet 194
Terrain: Pleasant, high-level walking across fields and through a plantation. This section of the route was opened in 1980.

Portesham, ¾ mile off the Path, has a grocer's shop, a public house, a post office and accommodation. Early closing day is Wednesday. The Manor House near the church was the home of Admiral Sir Masterman Hardy and dates from the seventeenth century.

The Hell Stone is a neolithic burial chamber which was incorrectly restored in the last century by some over-enthusiastic amateur archaeologists.

The 70-ft-high tower, erected in 1844, is a monument to Admiral Sir Thomas Masterman ('Kiss me') Hardy, Nelson's Flag Captain and life-long friend in whose arms he died at Trafalgar. The monument can be seen from many parts of Dorset.

Hardy was born in 1769 and first met Nelson when serving in the frigate *Meleager* as a lieutenant from 1793–4. He transferred to the *Minerve* (Nelson was the Commodore) and was put in charge of the prize *Sabina*. He was captured by the Spaniards

after a most gallant fight against overwhelming odds, but was soon exchanged and rejoined the fleet. In 1797, just before the battle of Cape St Vincent, the *Minerve* was chased by the Spanish fleet. A seaman fell overboard and Hardy launched the jolly boat to save him, but was in danger of being captured when Nelson backed his mizzen topsails declaring 'By God, I'll not lose Hardy', the Spaniards hesitated, fearing a trap, and Hardy was rescued. Later, he commanded the boats which cut out a French brig-of-war from under the guns of Santa Cruz and was immediately promoted by Earl St Vincent. After his retirement from active service he became governor of Greenwich Hospital and instituted many reforms, for he was a humane man who did all that was possible to relieve the miserable lot of the lower-deck sailor.

The area around the monument is a popular picnic spot and is a maze of paths. The views are superb.

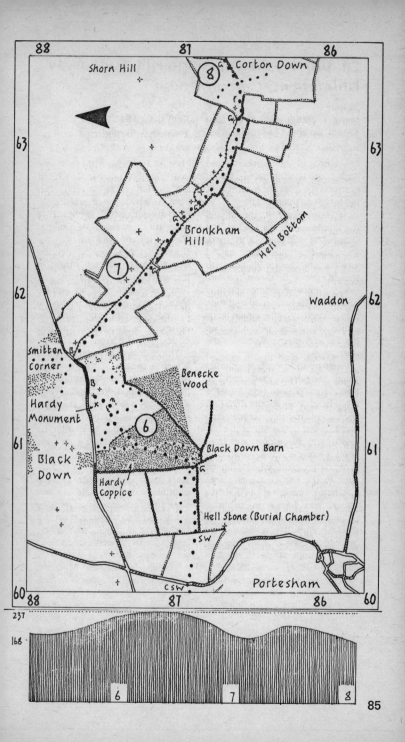

Shorn Hill

Corton Down

⑧

Bronkham Hill

Hell Bottom

⑦

Waddon

Smitten Corner

Benecke Wood

Hardy Monument

⑥

Black Down Barn

Black Down

Hardy Coppice

Hell Stone (Burial Chamber)

SW

CSW

Portesham

29. Corton Down, Ridge Hill, Ridgeway Hill, A354

2¾ miles
Maps: 1:25000 sheet SY68/78; 1:50000 sheet 194
Terrain: Splendid high-level walking with good views.

The whole of this section of the Path is littered with tumuli. To the north can be seen the magnificent hill fort of Maiden Castle.

At Ridgeway Hill, the official route follows the busy A354, the Dorchester to Weymouth road, for about ¼ mile. East-bound walkers who fear for life and limb should turn right down the old, roughly metalled road which runs parallel to the main road and then turn left across a stile which leads into a narrow field with a gate on the far side giving access to the A354.

West-bound walkers should cross the main road and go through the gate and make for the stile ahead. They should then turn right up the roughly metalled lane and turn left at the top of the hill.

Buses to Weymouth and Dorchester use the A354.

Maiden Castle, which can be seen to the north-east, is a vast earthwork covering 120 acres which was begun in neolithic times and greatly enlarged during the Iron Age. It was a centre of resistance against the Romans, whose troops under Vespasian stormed it in AD 43. In 1937, the Roman military cemetery was excavated and the skeletons of those who died in the battle were uncovered.

Dorchester (population 14,000), the Roman Durnovaria, and Casterbridge in the novels of Thomas Hardy, is a most attractive grey-stone town. Traces of the Roman walls can be seen from the walks, the beautiful tree-lined avenues which surround the town on three sides. At Colliton Park, the site of the County Council Offices, may be seen the best-preserved Roman house in Britain. Outside the town, the Romans constructed an amphitheatre in Maumbury Rings, a Bronze Age earthwork, and the defences were again fortified during the Civil War.

The church of St Peter is mainly fifteenth-century. Other interesting buildings include Judge Jeffrey's lodgings in High Street West, now a restaurant. It was in this Tudor building that the notorious judge stayed in 1685 after the Monmouth rebellion. At the 'Bloody Assize', 292 prisoners were sentenced to death and 80 were hanged, drawn and quartered. In the Old Crown Court the Tolpuddle Martyrs were sentenced to transportation for life in 1834 for administering illegal oaths in connection with trade-union activities.

The Dorset Military Museum, Bridport Road, houses a collection of militaria associated with various Dorset regiments, and the County Museum, next to St Peter's church, contains much material about Dorset as well as the Thomas Hardy room.

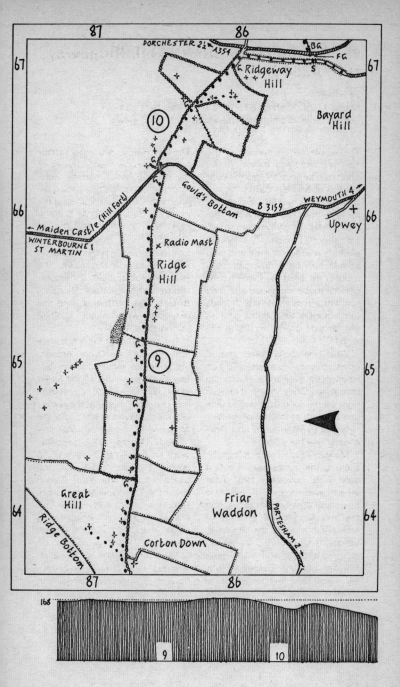

30. Ridgeway Hill, Came Wood, West Hill

2¼ miles
Maps: 1 : 25000 sheet SY68/78; 1 : 50000 sheet 194
Terrain: This section is mostly along the road and is not particularly interesting, although there are extensive views.

East-bound walkers will find little difficulty in following the route from the A354 until reaching the tip near mile 11. They should resist the natural temptation to follow the track which bears left uphill towards some buildings. Instead, they should pass through the gates on the other side of the track and follow the field edge, keeping the fence on the right, until reaching the road. This does not carry much traffic and is pleasant enough to walk along. Came Wood is probably the origin of Danver's Wood, described by Thomas Hardy in *The Trumpet-Major*, and Bincombe Hill is Overcombe Down.

West-bound walkers must leave the road at a gate opposite the notice warning the public to beware of golf balls. Those who end up in the tip have gone wrong and must retrace their steps to get to the other side of the fence.

There are numerous barrows and tumuli to be seen in the fields on either side of the route.

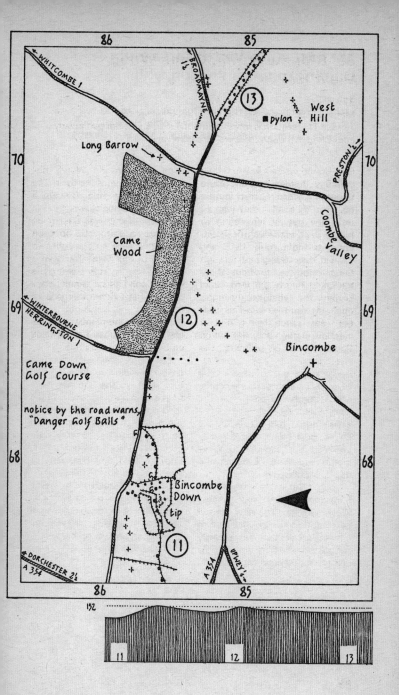

31. East Hill, White Horse Hill, Osmington, Osmington Mills

3 miles
Maps: 1:25000 sheet SY68/78; 1:50000 sheet 194
Terrain: There is good, fast walking over White Horse Hill and then a descent into Osmington. Osmington Mills is reached by field paths.

The Path follows the hill above the White Horse, which cannot be seen by east-bound walkers until they descend into the valley and turn round to look at it. It was cut into the turf in 1815 and shows King George III on his horse riding *away* from Weymouth. The irony is that the good citizens of Weymouth caused this chalk figure to be made to celebrate a visit from their monarch!

Below, in the valley, lies Sutton Poyntz, which is described as Overcombe in *The Trumpet-Major*. Hardy did not describe the village accurately and Overcombe Mill is probably based on the near-by Upwey Mill.

Osmington has a café, public house, post office, accommodation and bus services to Weymouth and Wool. Early closing day is Wednesday.

John Constable spent his honeymoon here and painted Weymouth Bay. The view can still be recognized. In the parish church of St Osmund, heavily restored in 1846, is a sixteenth-century monument with the fol- lowing curious inscriptions. The first, in Latin, translated reads: 'I have reached harbour. Farewell, hope and fortune – I have no more to do with you. Go sport with other people.' The next two are in English: 'Man's life. Man is a glas. Life is as water that is weakly walld about. Sinne brings in death. Death breaks the glas. So runnes the water out. Finis.' 'Here is not the man who in his life with every man had law and strife.'

East-bound walkers should leave the village on the A353 and turn right up the concrete farm road on the right-hand side of the road immediately after passing the derestriction sign. Where the farm road bears to the right continue forward through a gate into the field and bear left towards the far end of the field.

Osmington Mills has a seasonal grocer's shop on the caravan site, a public house, accommodation and bus services to Weymouth, Osmington and Wool.

Please turn to p. 56.

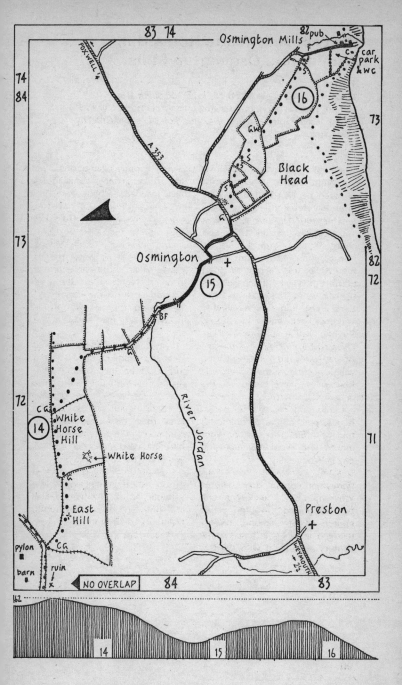

Index of Place Names

Index

Index

Index